'Bismil Laa Hir Rah Nᵃ

'In the name of God, most gracious, most merciful'

Self Help Guide to Meditation and The Quran

written by

ASIF SABA

Including more than 30 new affirmations and 5 meditation exercises

Published by Harvesting The Seeds Publications
For more information about this book, please contact the author
info@asifsabamindfulness.com
www.asifsabamindfulness.com

ISBN 978-0-9927999-7-7

Editor: Wendy Yorke
WRITE. EDIT. PUBLISH
www.wendyyorke.com

Cover Design – Jacqueline Abromeit
www.goodcoverdesign.co.uk

Proofreader – Paula Kench
www.bronteproofedit.co.uk

Verses used are from
The Meaning of the Illustrious Quran
By Allama Abdullah Yusuf Ali
First published in Lahore, Pakistan
in 1957 and reprinted in 1967.

Additional source information is from
The Holy Quran by Islamic researches (IFTA) printed at the King
Fahd printing complex
and
The Oxford Encyclopaedic English Dictionary

Dedication

To the reader

I thank you so much for inviting me into your life.

May you see beyond what is in this book and then write your own book (In Sha Allah). God Willing.

What you believe is impossible will become a possibility.

Additional Reading Coming soon

The Rock Crystals

A story inspired by true events.

Second book about **Meditation and *The Quran.***

Another journey into the mystical *Quran.*
This book has yet to receive its title.

Acknowledgements

I thank Allah for all the inspiration I received during the writing of this book. What I received gave me insights into the verses of *The Quran*. I give thanks for the guidance that brought me into contact with the following individuals.

To my Guardian Angels who have been so patient with me. This project has taken many years.

I thank Abdullah Yusuf Ali, who translated *The Quran* from Arabic to English. His work has made this book possible.

To Paul, Tasneem, Aska and Durga who were among the first to read this final edition.

Wendy Yorke
I thank Wendy. She is an amazing editor. She saw what the writing needed and gave it a clearer voice. Without her skills and guidance, the book would not shine so much.
www.wendyyorke.com

Special thanks to Paula Kench who proofread the book before publication.
www.bronteproofedit.co.uk

Special thanks to Jacqueline Abromeit
www.goodcoverdesign.co.uk

Foreword

In a world where there are numerous voices instructing us in the way to go, very few of them point to the inner way with such truth. They tell us to trust in money, institutions and even exterior forms of worship. Even those who teach the practice of meditation, will often focus on some physical or superficial benefit of the ancient discipline. We are taught that it only dwells in certain buildings and temples, or that we must be of a certain religion to have any hope of being a part of something greater than ourselves. Is it any wonder that many have abandoned the road of religion, and have taken the path of selfish humanism or materialism?

If the spiritual history of the human race teaches us anything, it is that in such times of great intellectual darkness and chaos, the true teachers will begin to rise from our cultures. In my humble and heartfelt opinion, Mr. Asif Saba is one of those teachers. In his book, The Self-help Guide to Meditation and *The Quran*, you will be guided on a journey of meditation and the metaphysical. You will learn how to break free of those exterior, material forms that seem to loom so large in our current world. You will be instructed on how to break away from those damaging inner voices that keep you trapped on the wheel of perpetual misery and self-sabotage. Moreover, perhaps most importantly of all, you will uncover the divine presence that resides lovingly within your own heart. Through practical meditation exercises, you will discover that sacred space within known as the inner sacred mosque.

The Self-help Guide to Meditation and *The Quran* is a true, spiritual gem that is a must-read for anyone on the path of self-discovery. It goes beyond divisions and religious borders, and seeks to unite us all in the unity of divine love. It dismisses any superstitions or misgivings that the reader might have about *The Holy Quran* and opens our eyes to the deep, metaphysical wisdom of this ancient text. This book is a very timely call for each of us to take steps and go beyond the lines that divide us all. No more can we assume the us-and-them mentality that this world of Illusion has superimposed on our consciousness. It is time that we begin to live from the depths of our inner selves, where our exterior conflicts dissolve and each of us begins to evolve. In these pages, you will find gentleness and wisdom that will help you on that inner journey. In addition, that gentleness and wisdom is authentic, because what you read in these words reflects the wisdom, intelligence and gentleness of their author. Asif Saba is truly one of the hidden sages of our time, and I am truly honoured to endorse his book to the world. I am also extremely honoured to call him friend.... The inner mosque awaits your entry! Paul James Caiden

Praise for this Book

"*Self Help Guide to Meditation and The Quran* is a true, undiscovered gem in the metaphysical field and should be read by any serious student, as well as seasoned teachers. Asif Saba is the real deal and you can feel his authenticity in every sentence of the book. Definitely a work and an author that should be greatly supported." Paul James Caiden, author of *An Angel Came Down*

"An amazing book full of insights. A must read. This book has changed my life by opening my mind and making me think and practice on a more personal level. I have read all the books by Asif and would recommend them to anyone who is looking for some guidance and understanding in life." Tasneem Hussain, Graduate of Law (LLB LPC)

"A book full of hidden gems and treasures that will guide you to a much-needed enlightened path. Every time you read it something new will stand out and pierce your heart and soul. You must read it and practice with an open and willing mind and it will speak to you in magical tones. It will show you a place within Islam where you feel you belong. I feel privileged to have come across this book and the wise words of wisdom that speak to me. It has taught me the importance of meditation in Islam and how we need to revive the teachings of our prophet and Allah." Aska Karem - Artist/Author of a book called Halima

"This book is one of the best books I have read about Meditation. I truly love the book. I will be recommending it to my friends. The author's work is amazing. He explains many things about meditation and spirituality. I learned a lot reading this book and started practicing meditation." Durga Lakshmi – Health Administration

About the Author

Asif is an author and musician. His books are ground-breaking, his music inspirational. Those who have read his books have had their lives transformed. They give the reader insights into *The Quran*. You will become fascinated by its mystical messages. Its words of wisdom will expand your way of looking at what you already understand.

As an author, Asif will take you on a journey, helping you to see with vision and clarity. His books offer you guidance and help. He explains to you the spiritual and mystical messages within *The Quran* to help you on your meditative journey.

Contents

Introduction: My Story

My first memory of having a spiritual experience was at the age of five. I turned around and saw a bright yellow light. The only thing I knew about this light was that it came down from heaven. To this day, I still remember it. My next experience was at the age of ten. Remembering this experience continues to create a smile for me. I was running around a table in the house where I lived and in a single moment, there was a strange feeling that came over me. My mind then filled with a vision of the universe. This made me stop running and look at what I was seeing and then it was gone. It only lasted for a few seconds but at the time, it actually felt longer. From that moment, little pieces of information about events in the future showed up on the screen of my mind as visions. Knowing about events before they happened was very strange at that age. They continued to happen, now and again, for a couple of years then all of a sudden, they stopped for a while.

The next major experience happened around the age of thirteen years old. This was a visitation from a spiritual being. Although there was no one in the room, the spirit's energy was everywhere. I felt its gentle eyes on me. The experience only lasted a short time and then it faded away. As I reflect back on the visitation, I now know, my father came to visit me on that memorable night. You may be asking yourself, "What is the big deal about your father coming into your room". My father had passed away ten years previously. Other experiences at that age were in the form of dreams about angels and prophets. It is amazing how these spiritual experiences can stay with you for the rest of your life. I guess it is because they were so out of the ordinary.

When I was engaged in some Earthly activity, I would also experience a speeding up process, a quickening, an elevating of my consciousness. Everything seen through my physical eyes became small, like looking at the world through binoculars. The things in front of me became distant rather than near. I could feel an energy swirling around me when this happened. It was like being inside of something, looking out. There was also a knowing that everything was fine, without knowing anything.

Telling other people about these experiences was not a welcome topic. At such a young age, I relied on the older generation to have all the answers to my questions. But they could not answer these questions. These experiences continued to happen. At the time, I thought that there were no answers to my questions. The conclusion I reached about the experiences was that they were a strange thing to happen to someone. I remember thinking; some people have stomach-aches, others headaches, other people go to hospital when they become ill. I figured these experiences were one of those things that happened; that they were a part of growing up and getting older in life. That they happened to everyone but they did not talk about them. The world became a more attractive place to play in rather than the strange things I experienced, so I acknowledged them and left it at that. After all, the physical world was here and now.

At eighteen years of age, I was living in a house shared by many different people, one of whom played the guitar. We became friends and when he moved on, he gave me his old guitar. Learning to play this instrument was a truly enjoyable experience. Creating and playing music brought with it a new way of hearing. Creating music took me into a different space. It was a little bit like saying a prayer or meditation. Prayer can take you to the door, however, meditation is the opening of the door and walking through it. The creation of music allowed me to use thought processes in a different way. It gave me something creative to do. I did not understand it then but sometimes when I was playing the guitar, colours would imprint themselves on the screen of my mind when I played certain cords. When I played music, there were times when I heard it on a spiritual level. The melodies in my head transformed into actual sound. Playing and hearing music like this was not like listening to music through the radio or record players. The music within is in perfect harmony and pitch. As I walked down the street or sat on the bus, music would all of a sudden start playing in my head. I knew nobody else could hear it. While this was happening, I would become like a conductor. Whatever melody I thought about was right there. The spiritual music I heard came through the mind, rather than with my physical ears. Whole orchestras could be added to the music. Heavenly choirs, lead and backing vocals accompanied the tune. When I got home and tried to recreate what I had heard in my head. I would spend all day playing the guitar hoping to bring it out. However, this was not to be the case. Now and again, I would connect and bring something out but this only lasted a brief moment.

After a couple of years learning to play the guitar, a vocal coach gave me instructions on how to sing. Learning to control my breathing was one of the exercises given to help with tone, length and balance of notes. Learning to control my breathing became a regular practice. I would lie on my bed with my eyes closed. Taking a deep breath, I would exhale the air as slowly as possible. I did this as a way of learning to control the speed the air was released by my lungs. As I did this, I could feel my heart beating within my chest. This led to me thinking about slowing down my heartbeat to help me with the breathing exercise. After a number of weeks practicing, I had an out of body experience. I believe this was due to the slowing down of my heartbeat. On one occasion, I floated up and bumped into the ceiling. The floating sensation made me open my eyes. I looked at my physical body lying there on the bed. It was a strange experience, of which we will explore in more detail in my second book.

Each person has some kind of belief about Heaven. However, an out of body experience changes everything you think you know. The beautiful truth about such an experience is that it reveals how we remain the same person. We do not all of a sudden change into an angel. You are you, but without the limitations of a physical body.

Returning to my body, I realised how damp, wet, and heavy it felt compared to my spiritual self. How limited we are in awareness as we reside within it.

As I got older, learning more about life and the world made me search for answers about my spiritual experiences. By the time I was twenty-five, I had read a number of books that answered some of my questions. From then on, my life was never the same. Meditation became an important part of my daily life. Through meditation, I worked to expand my conscious awareness and during the next five years, I learnt so much.

I have had many life changing experiences during my inner moments of meditation. I became aware there are other ways in which we can communicate. That thoughts are not only ideas running around in your head, they become manifest. Sometimes, I would hear other people's thoughts; feel their illnesses and spiritual conditions. I have also been shown what some people dreamed about the previous night. We have the ability to communicate with the animal kingdom. Truly, animals have thoughts and feelings. They have spirits and it is our duty as the dominant consciousness in this world to treat them as spiritual beings and look after them with love. They are a creation of God and they too are on their spiritual journey. *The Quran* explains this in *Sura 6 Verse* 38.

Reaching the age of about thirty-four, curiosity led me to reading *The Quran*. This was another major learning and turning point. It was around 1992. Reading *The Quran,* took my understanding to a new level. When I reached *Sura 45 Verse 12,* I had a feeling of inspiration surging all around me. It was impressed on me that I had not fully understood what I was reading. There was another way to understanding the meaning behind the verses. Up to that point, I had related all that I had read to the physical world. Through inspiration, it was revealed that *The Quran* should not be read with your attention focused on the physical reality. Instead I should focus on the higher wisdom contained within the verses. It was also impressed on me that I should see myself as a ship sailing through the sea. Now that it was made clear to me about how I should understand the verses, I thought to myself, 'Why did I not see this earlier?' I remembered reading many verses in *The Quran* that spoke about ships sailing and this really piqued my need to know more. I remember sighing and thinking to myself, 'Once I have finished reading *The Quran,* I am going to have to read it again'. I stood up, went to the shop, and bought a pen and book with lined paper. Looking at *The Quran* and the way it was written, I drew lines down the blank pages of the book I had brought. I was going to reference all the interesting verses I found. Back from the shop, I returned to reading *The Quran.* I started taking notes of chapter, verses and snippets of verses. Over a three-year period, I read *The Quran* back-to-back, many times, writing down verses of interest to me. Notes were made next to each verse. There were pages and pages of references. It was around that time computers were becoming popular. It was not too long after that I bought a second-hand computer. I typed out all the notes I had made and then typed out the whole of *The Quran* from start to finish. As the notes I was making grew, I started to categorise them under headings. Through inspiration, these gems of wisdom formed a firm foundation of knowledge within me. They gave me a greater spiritual insight about myself and the journey I was on.

Over the years, I have had many spiritual experiences. These include, seeing spirits and speaking with those who have departed from this world, speaking with the animal kingdom, hearing people's thoughts, knowing the events of the past and future, visiting other worlds, connecting to and being aware of the consciousness of the prophets. Knowing of the different stations we consciously connect to and many other experiences.

How to Use this Book

The *Sura* (chapter and verses) used in this book highlight gems of wisdom I have found meaningful. The aim of this book is to help you on your journey. As you apply *The Quran's* words of wisdom, you will be inspired to listen, not only with your physical ears, but to your own inspired feelings. Through meditation, you can raise your consciousness and experience the wonders and delights the hereafter has to offer you.

You are a spiritual being with a physical body. You have a form, called a spirit that transcends this physical world. As you awaken, you can use your struggles to your advantage. This book explains simple and beautiful truths and experiences you may face as you work to awaken your awareness. Its aim is to teach you and fill you with hope and love in readiness for when you are called to account. There is a world that exists beyond the veil that separates the physical and the spiritual worlds. As you accept the incoming information, you will stand firm as you sail your ship through your own experiences.

It is my honour to share with you this book, that it might help you and give you many beautiful insightful words of wisdom to help you advance on your journey. It is a mixture of my true-life experiences and what has been sent to me as inspiration. It is my wish that you find what is here helpful to your own journey of awakening.

Chapter 1: Meditation and *The Quran*

The Quran is a book from God, which contains 114 *Suras* (chapters). An interpretation of its verses can be viewed either through loving, meditative insights or clothed in a vision about the movement of matter, and its comings and goings to and from this physical world. This book will focus on an interpretation that brings the verses to life as you peer into the depth of your inner spiritual self. In the world of physical form, you plant seeds in the garden and watch them grow. Each seed has all that it needs within it to grow and complete its cycle of life. You are a seed encased in a shell and you contain all you need to complete your life's journey.

The Quran entered our world through the Prophet Muhammad (please repeat to yourself 'Peace Be Upon Him', each time his name is mentioned in this book and also that of other prophets) around 1442 years ago, via the Archangel Gabriel. This was by means of clairvoyance and clairaudience. It started in the cave of Hira. This is a place where the Prophet Muhammad secluded himself away from everyone and meditated. What is here will take you on that same meditative journey. From the first *Quranic* revelation to the last, it was 22 years, 5 months and 14 days before the verses of *The Quran* were completed.

This book contains verses from *The Quran* and meditation exercises for you, as well as clarification about the experiences you may have on your journey. *The Quran* quoted is an old English version, translated by Yusuf Ali from Arabic to English. The verses used in this book may have more than one verse referenced. For example, *Sura 21, Verses 16-18*, however, only verse 18 or part of that verse will be in this book. Use your own *Quran* for additional reading to gain a fuller understanding. If there is a quote that does not match up exactly with the version that you have, it may be a different edition. The insights here about *The Quranic* verses will help you unravel the mysteries you have yet to discover about yourself. Through the thoughts you construct and the information contained within *The Quran*, you go on a journey as you travel into your spiritual self's unlimited depths.

The word Islam means, *surrender* and as you ponder about its meaning, remember Islam is a state of mind, not a state-of-the-art building. As you live your life and look within, what is reflecting on the screen of your mind comes through your inner self. It is in this reflection that you construct and draw a meaning from the verses of *The Quran*.

The Quranic verses explain the detailed steps of a pathway. They take you on a journey into the mysteries that lie behind all action and reaction within your inner self and the physical world. The inner pathway is a journey filled with wonder. You will discover that there is a rhythmic pattern between yourself and the verses. As you ponder on the reflection within the mind, you bring to life the eyes of your inner self. From the Heavens to your inner self, seeds fall to the ground. Some of the seeds firmly plant themselves in the garden of your inner self. Others fall into the sea and the waves of conflicting thought activity that ruffles the surface wash them away.

It is not until you look at something with an open heart that you can see the open way. Clear your mind of any preconceived ideas about what you expect to find. If you are not happy with something, it may not be because it does not contain truth. You need to look at the hallucination, programmed conditioning that is traumatising you. Listen to the beautiful melodies that sing to you through your inner light. As you inwardly reflect, you will find the greatest truths in the smallest thoughts you think.

It is inevitable that we will change as we awaken to the truth the prophets came to teach. Nothing in life stays static but it moves; pulsating; vibrating; and expanding. We too, must learn to expand with the rhythms and harmonic accordance of life, as the Spiritual Laws influence and impress themselves on us, according to our deeds and spiritual needs. An understanding about the Spiritual

Laws will become clear as you continue to read. Accepting change is a sign that you have not closed the windows and drawn the curtains to the inspiration that comes from the Heavens.

Sura 13 Verse 11
11. Verily never will God change the condition of a people until they change it themselves (with their own souls).

Wisdom is the intelligence behind all wise thoughts. The reason you are reading this book is with the intention to know or learn something new. What is in the following pages is not about changing the outer world. It is about helping you to rediscover the godly qualities within yourself. Much of what you have previously learnt, even what you think you know, may be no more than a partial truth when spiritual wisdom is placed by its side. Let this wisdom take you on a journey far beyond the day-to-day reality where you live. When you turn your vision inward towards the inner light, you reduce the pull the three-dimensional world has on you. You can learn to bring Heaven to Earth instead of hoping to take Earth to Heaven.

One reason why there are many interpretations of spiritual insights and philosophies is that we as individuals, with freewill, create, construct, make up and accept information according to our inner awareness. As you discuss and exchange thoughts, through an inner dialogue, the facts as you see them, influence and shape you on your pathway. Some of the verses of *The Quran* include guidance about your spiritual and physical needs simultaneously. Contemplation will help you to find your way through the conjecture thrown up by irregularities. When you find yourself comparing one irregular thought pattern against another, the result will not create a truth. When your irregular thoughts are all you have to drive you along, your conclusions about your experiences appear true because you believe they are happening to you. You may understand this when you realise, things happen and exist because you think them so. To reach the inner sacred mosque, look for the pathway that leads you through the things you believe are happening to you.

The journey back to God needs very little physical action. It is not what you do, but the reason behind what you think, that stimulates spiritual growth. With awareness must come the ability to reason. The use of your ability to reason is the key to unlocking the mysteries within, thus opening the door to the secrets contained within *The Quran.*

As you begin to see and know through inspirational thoughts, you can choose to co-operate with the truth or you can reject it. If persuaded, you decide to move among your irregularities, what will follow is a wave of disruption and chaos. When you realise how your irregularities interrupt your spiritual journey, turn your back on them, look to new horizons and hold your vision steady.

When you read *The Quran* what you see within the verses will depend on the interior of your spiritual self. Entering a state of loving kindness will elevate you to a degree where you will see the beautiful reality of *The Quran.* When you create thoughts of mischief, you drastically reduce your vision and insight, cutting yourself off from the flow of wisdom and inspiration that advises you.

If you let your perception cloud with mischief and insecurities, the verses will appear unintelligible, unrelated and confusing. Do not underestimate the true power of love and its ability to bring clarification to the verses of *The Quran.*

Put your trust in the inspiration that comes to you. Wisdom in its highest form is the recognition and acceptance of trust and truth. As the best of your thoughts arise, they burst forth bringing with them a light by which you can see. It is for you to meditate and go beyond the baseline of thoughts that plague your mind. Loving wisdom allows you to walk your journey smoothly. By always improving your ideas, updating them through wisdom and inspiration, you will change the content of your inner self. To do this you need to identify the programmes of conditioning influencing the way you see and interpret your evidence and experiences. As your loving thoughts of wisdom become your foundation, you will begin to change the conditions under which you live.

 You start to become independent when you reason things out for yourself. Look beyond your immediate reality. All you experience during any kind of meditation is God's way of letting you know that He is with you. He is ready and able to respond to your requests as you go within. If you do not see or detect the presence of anything, it does not mean you have not received. Meditation is like anything else you do. It takes practise before you experience the results consciously. It is through applied intention, persistence and steadfastness that you begin to make an inner connection. You will begin to feel, know and see beyond the reality of irregularity. With your permission, God's angels will help you to change the irregular activities that plague and disrupt your divine patterning. To help you, repeat affirmations daily, such as the following:

The light that shines from deep within
Will realign my true patterning.
From head to toe, above and below.
Oh light, align my soul.

 You can repeat these words of wisdom, saying them like a *zikr*; a remembrance of God, through the repetition of a word, or sentences in praise of God. In this book, there are numerous exercises, choose those you feel will help you most. You can also make your own up or seek them out elsewhere. It is all about finding what works for you and going with the flow. When you work the affirmations, let there be a harmonisation between the thoughts in your mind and the sound of your voice. This will create a powerful vibration that will resonate throughout your whole self.

Thoughts make things happen. They also help you to identify and create a meaning and purpose to your life. Instead of having aims and ambitions that only fulfil Earthly desires, let your feelings act as little antennae. Feel them reach out their hands. Let them bring into your life a greater wisdom and vision.

Through the eyes of love, let the verses of *The Quran* inspire you by way of reason. As they do, you will begin to perceive an in-depth insight into what they say. Where once you thought, 'What does this mean?' You begin to see the verses unfolding. As you do, the old must give way to the new as the winds of spiritual energy around you change. The awareness of men and women will develop. Inspiration will bring with it a greater influx of truth about *The Quranic* verses. Blockages that have limited your awareness will no longer be a hindrance. Within you, a doorway is always open through which God's love and wisdom flows.

Sura 21 Verse 18
18. Nay, we hurl the truth against falsehood, and it knocks out its brain, and behold, falsehood doth perish!

Behind all things created, behind everything that happens there is a reason. Behind all reasons, God resides. Learn to appreciate what reason is. Reason is a powerful influence. You can also choose what you do through your reason.

Each one of us is here on probation. We have come here to learn through experience. *Sura 21 Verse 16* explains we are not here to play leapfrog with each other in a bid to climb the hierarchy of wealth and status. Nor, has the world been set up as a people's playground.

One way to find the answers to questions concerning life is to listen. Become familiar with the workings in your life of the Spiritual Laws, which govern us all.

The questions you find yourself asking might include the following:

1. How is the balance between my polarity maintained?

2. Why does the darkness not quickly overcome the light, although at times it may look that way?

3. What is it about my interactions with other people, followed by my reactions; how does this determine my fate?

You will find the answers to these questions in this book. It does not take great skill to make better judgements and understand the Spiritual Laws that shape our destiny. There are many Spiritual Laws that govern all of us, the following are examples only.

Spiritual Laws

- The Law of Cause and Effect
- The Law of Polarity
- The Law of Attraction
- The Law of Equality
- The Law of Freewill
- The Law of Abundance

Never underestimate the precision of God's Spiritual Laws. As you explore the inner depths of your spiritual self, you will unlock the awareness of how best to work with these laws. Spiritual Laws are those that apply themselves to and govern all life. These laws are not like the laws of our physical world that can change from country to country. The laws of the world are usually in line with our moral codes of conduct. However, our morals and codes of conduct change.

Chapter 2: The Three Veils

In this chapter we explore an example of how our experiences can help us see truth through reason. Also, we will investigate the three veils. We have all, at some point in our life, met someone for who we have felt respect. When you hear or directly experience a side to that person outside of your pre-conceived ideas, it can change your perception of them. Was the respect you had a truth or falsehood?

There are different types of respect. One flows from the truth while the others are a creation constructed from irregularities. False respect is to admire someone because of their appearance, social or economic status. This type of respect is more to do with envy. The kind of respect that stands alone is the one based on surrender. The greatest respect you can hold within is when, in truth and trust, you feel humble before God and humanity.

Imagine watching a colony of ants as they go about their daily life. As you watch, you are a part of the activity, yet you are not. Looking at the ants, you think how similar they are to the way we are. Each ant has a life, a purpose, a destiny to fulfil. In that moment of contemplation, let your feelings expand. The feelings of respect you feel for life and God's creation will rise up within you. This respect will not diminish but increase as you continue to explore nature and the rest of God's creation.

We do not always see truth straight away. As you think about different types of respect, does this not make you wonder what other ideas you have decided to incorporate into your life that cloud your vision? If having respect for someone was in truth, it would last forever. It does not change its form when confronted by certain patterns of behaviour. Look at each human being you meet. Think to yourself that this person is a creation of God. Attached to the physical body is a spirit that has come into this world as a part of God's divine plan. Once the spirit's experiences are completed, it returns to the Heavens having accomplished this stage of its journey. Each of us is like a piece of the jigsaw. We each fit, each one of us a part of God's divine plan, creating a perfect picture.

Listen to your wisdom, paying attention to new ways of expressing yourself. Develop the ability to remove anything that fools you into believing something is true when it is not. As you strive to recognise spiritual truths, you will free yourself from the things that blind you. The complex rules by which we live may take a lifetime to show up as burdens in our lives. When they do, be aware and make that change. The physical world is not the illusion; it is a dense spiritual state. The illusions start with the thoughts you create when unconditional love is not your foundation.

Sura 16 Verse 96
96. What is with you must vanish: what is with God will endure.

It does not take much effort to recognise falsehood: only a few moments of self-reflection and an honest mindset. The old you will vanish and a new you will emerge. Unless you allow a self-generated loving change of thought activity to step forward, you will find yourself jumping between truth and irregular thoughts of imagined activity.

Sura 27 Verse 14
14. Though their souls were convinced thereof.

The process of change takes place with the help of wisdom. Every small change adds to the multitude of changes we each need to make. If you are one of the lucky ones who catch hold of a piece of truth, do not bury it beneath old ideas. Hold on to it, allow it to grow, develop and expand. Even if your mind rejects truth, your inner self will accept it. If you cover truth up, one day it will arise seeking its rightful place within your life. God and the angels come to you through the truth and trust that you feel. Follow these feelings before irregularity interferes.

Slowly the truths will devour the falsehoods. The best way to remain in truth is to seek out the source of the original thought of truth. This will help you keep a truer internal balance. If you were to ask where this thought or that thought came from, the reply would be, 'Where were you standing when the thought entered your mind?' Later, this statement will become clearer, as you think about the different states or degrees of conscious awareness you experience. Another way to look at where you are consciously residing is through your mood swings. They reflect your different states of consciousness. As you turn your attention within, what exists there shows up on the screen of your mind.

On your journey, you have a choice. The untruth hinders you, making your journey slow. If you follow a middle course, you will find yourself forever wandering between truth and untruth. One moment you are ascending to the heights of all that is good, the next moment you are descending into all that self-sabotages you. You perceive your action, not paying too much attention to its consequences. Then, there are people with whom God is well pleased.

We live within multiple degrees of conscious activity. We choose the one that suits our fleeting desires. This is according to the beliefs we hold at that moment about our destiny. As the irregular hallucinogenic programmes become a reality in our mind, they enforce a perception of reality on us. These visions and thought programmes flutter from one person to another, generation after generation. They cloud each new spirit's awareness of its inner reality and unity with God.

Sura 39 Verse 6
6. He created you (all) from a single person ...
He makes you, in the wombs of your mothers, in stages, one after another, in three veils of darkness.

The Quran and your inner truth will reveal to you that we did not only spring up and evolve. To cut a long story short, we descended from the spiritual realms into the physical. We were living a life as a spiritual being in the spiritual world, with garments according to our inner expression. The command went forth and we arrived on planet Earth.

It does not matter where we first appeared on the face of the Earth. Its population has been through many changes as civilisations have dominated its surface. Hardly a trace of their existence remains except for the few scattered fragments you find hidden beneath the surface.

The world on which we congregate is but a dense form of a spiritual expression. Our thoughts determine how we face our challenges. We are here to experience, learn and transform into light, the base matter into which we are born. To do this, it is important that you listen to the voice of your Guardian angel. You may know this better as the voice of your conscience.

The former verse talks about three veils of darkness. The three veils that drastically reduce you experiencing the light and love of God are: certain types of thinking; your negative emotions, which should not be taken for an expression of your feelings; and your willpower. Firstly, thinking in its base matter form shows up as your negative thoughts. These thoughts come from your tribal self and its dark crowd. Secondly, emotions and not any emotional activity, your negative emotions. They add to your construction of negative thoughts and create sensations of instability. Emotional discord will distract and distort your spiritual vision. Lastly, there is willpower or the lack of it. When you are emotionally distraught, you can lose the will to go on. This lack of willpower makes you weak. The pains you experience through negative thoughts drain you of willpower and they bring you down.

12

By learning to use your feelings, which should not be taken for an expression of negative emotional activity, you expand your awareness. As loving thoughts flow, they fill you with feelings of love. This raises your consciousness in the direction of the Heavens and you experience an expansion of your awareness. The content of this loving energy enhance and strengthen your willpower and you feel stronger and more confident. Instead of letting yourself be directed by your tribal self, you are guided by the wisdom that flows through your evolved self. As you become empowered, as you reach c   ith love, an amazing change surrounding your mindset will tal   ome a dweller in a land on high. Your loving emoti   They are the place through which you r   what is gathered and expa   ot activate your fee   er-development of yo   you have no control. Th   sails of your ship.

people that are loss *allergia* ✗

                                        further and travel the
                                        use you have learnt to
experience,   using your emotions, it does not mean their enforce   on is the only reality. Through your feelings, a greater truth reveals itself whereas your negative emotions can blur your vision. Use your feelings to make a connection with what lies behind the immediate idea in front of you.

Learning to distinguish the difference between your feelings and emotions is all part of the spiritual journey. They are a part of you, so you have to listen to yourself, carefully, distinguishing the difference between their approaches to life. Feelings of love turn a ruffled sea into a beautiful calm sea.

Inspiration from your angels and loved ones offering you guidance finds its way to you. Do not allow irregularity to step in and cast a shadow of doubt. Be prepared to accept whatever truth comes to you. As you expand your feelings, you will realise they are the doorway to the Heavens and your inspired understandings. Do you choose and make the irregularities your door to the hereafter? Alternatively, do you choose to make a difference and go through the door to your greatest love, truth and trust?

Certain characteristics found in the garden of the inner self can hinder you. They express themselves in you as attitudes. By using constructive criticisms, spend a little time thinking about how you can change the following conditions under which you live.

- Your attitude towards wanting to learn.
- Your attitude towards your experiences in life.
- Your attitude adjusting to the two above.
- Your attitude towards the concept of time.

Do not condition yourself, believing that you are too old to start learning. This leads to the creation of more attitudes. When you take away the time factor, you have all the time you need. Look at your fears, constructing a way to deal with them. They are but fragmented impressions that oppress you. They are but an illusion. Each of these attitudes above is a state of mind, conditioning. Your ability to create thoughts allows you to make changes that cancel out irregular activity.

Your negative attitudes limit you from expressing and experiencing your feelings to the full. Through your feelings, you become aware of God's truth. Better for you, is your understanding through your feelings. How many times in your life have you proven that you are greater than you give yourself credit? It is good to remember a situation in your life where you proved to yourself that you could accomplish the task. When you find yourself struggling and need a boost of self-confidence, step into that moment of success. You are not a failure because within you is the potential to be great. Entering a state of loving surrender allows you to withdraw yourself from the negative emotions about the manifest matter. You can get through any experience when you surrender because all things have a beginning and an end. As you work with wisdom, it sustains you on your journey, be that journey short or long. Here is another inspired affirmation for you to use daily.

Inside of me there is room for change.
To cleanse my house and rearrange.
The thoughts and images that manifest.
That my spirit's light will shine its best.

As a way of further helping you to understand this gathering of thoughts, be aware that within you, there are three main states of consciousness, including: the conscious self, subconscious self, and the unconscious self. The tribal self seeks to fill you with irregularities. The evolved self seeks to grow and develop you in the direction of the light. Both of these provide you with something to delight you. It is through the evolved self that you receive the best inspiration and guidance.

Each of your major conscious states has a greater vision than the one preceding it. Each conscious state has many degrees within its polarity. The total number of degrees between man and God is seventy thousand. You live and cycle through a small proportion of these degrees and around these states. The Spiritual Law of Polarity governs each one of us. You will have an idea about where you are residing within your polarity by the way you feel. Thoughts and images from the different degrees imprint themselves in your mind. As they do, truth and trust will be there to preside over each thought or set of thoughts you think.

One way of expanding your overall consciousness is to start having an honest dialogue with yourself. This will open the pathway to the greater conscious states. Start by listening when wisdom suggests a truth to you. The more you listen the more you will hear wisdom's voice, amid the turmoil of other thoughts. Within the greater states of consciousness are all the answers you need to help you find your way into its surroundings. When you take the irregular thoughts that arise and measure them against the content of the subconscious or unconscious, you will realise how small in stature they are. When irregularities impress their content on you, they will indeed seem larger than life. However, in the greater degrees of consciousness, you will experience a deeper depth and a wider breadth to your awareness. The irregularities that exist within you as an overwhelming force are but a speck in lands that are clean and good.

If you are not listening inwardly, when the light activity enters your immediate consciousness to advise you, it will be as a cloud passing by.

Unless you learn to listen and separate yourself from the irregularities that show up, you will have no choice but to believe in the perception they present to you. You will find the land of irregularities is a lonely place to reside compared to the other lands you can visit. The build-up of irregular activity that occurs clouds the door to wisdom, limiting your ability to hear the full measure of the inspiration sent to liberate and free you. When surrounded by irregular patterns of activity, life can appear to be a battleground due to the self-sabotaging, self-inflicted thoughts that attack the wisdom of your greater self. The events that take place within, shape your perception as your life unfolds. Activate your feelings of love and listen to the wisdom. As you do, you will expand your awareness, developing yourself towards your greatest spiritual potential.

Take to the sea and learn to swim beyond the reach of the irregularities. To help you on your journey, you perceive duality in the conscious self, because it is able to reflect the light and the darkness. Too much negative emotional activity will increase your irregular perception. Your negative emotions are active in the way they are because you activated them during your interactions in the physical world. By listening to your feelings, you will increase their activity, helping to balance the activity of your emotions. Your feelings will enhance your intuition about matters and you will gain a clearer insight. Use your feelings the next time you go shopping. Before you choose a particular item, get a feel for it. Extend your feelings, open your intuition, and be in the moment with the object of your attention. Explore how you really feel about buying that particular item. Your feelings will let you know if the object of your attention is for you. If it is not right for you, choose another one. It could be that the first item you picked had an unwanted attachment, problem or fault, you could not physically see. You might need a little practice. However, as your feelings actively develop, you will begin to know. This is the beginning stages of your awareness opening. As you continue to do this, you will instinctively know, on seeing an item, if it is for you or not. As you work with your innate abilities, your awareness will expand. If you do not use your feelings, they will remain undeveloped, making your journey through life a struggle.

Awareness Exercise

- Pick up an object, focus your attention on your feelings and expand your awareness.
- Feel yourself connect to what you are holding.
- Include your mental power and thinking and see what images flash on the screen of your mind.
- Let the object in your hand speak to your inner self.
- Listen to your feelings of intuition, they are a doorway to opening your awareness.

Chapter 3: *Muraqabah*; Meditation

Sura 38 Verse 29
29. Here is ... a book which we have sent down unto thee full of
blessings, that they may meditate on its signs.

The pathway we must all travel has been tried, tested and proven true by many who travel its highway. It is that of muraqabah, or meditation.

This can have a different meaning for each of us. It is the practice of the ability to withdraw from the irregularities that arise within the mind. To help us attain an inner state of peace, we focus on creating and holding ourselves within a single expression of love, because in love there are no irregularities. To do this we use our thinking and reasoning power; our feelings to guide us; and our willpower to hold us steady.

There are numerous ideas held about people who meditate. One idea is they are running around in life with flowers in their hair singing la-de-da songs and acting as though they have lost their grip on reality. Meditation does not mean you must take yourself off to a remote place in the woods. This type of thinking is nothing but conjecture. However, quietness cuts down on distractions and helps you focus. This is why the prophet Muhammad would seclude himself away in the cave of Hira and meditate. Through an inner focus, you learn to direct and hold your consciousness in the direction of the sacred mosque. For those of you unsure where the first sacred mosque is, it is within you. Strive to reach this place of great beauty and from there say your prayers. In your stillness, you will start to detect the flow of energy around you, using your own energy.

As you express feelings of love, you attract the attention of God and the angelic forces. Within you is a place you can visit seeking to establish a connection through which you can converse with the angelic angels in the afterlife. You must create the right conditions within yourself. As you detect the direction along which you should flow, you realise, through your inner light, you will find your own spiritual salvation. Through the light, you receive inspiration and mystical knowledge. In the light, you will find security from irregularities.

Each of us will reach a point in our spiritual evolution where we find the material world exerts less of an influence on us. Until that time arrives, we need what the world has to offer. We are mentally thrown around as we learn through experience to humble ourselves. As you repair the damage through the expression of love, do not reject others you meet because they lack the strength to remain on the path you believe is true. This is not acting from a position of love. Without them, you would not be where you are today. Who else could teach you what you need to learn? All the people in your life are a reflection of your past, present and future. They bring to the surface what hides within, so you can work on it. Instead of looking outwards, turn the eyes inwards. The practice of *muraqabah* helps you to hold yourself steady within the light that manifests. Ideally, to meditate it is best to choose the quietest room in the house, preferably one that is the least used. A preference as to the lighting conditions will differ from person to person. Some people prefer a dark or dimly lit room while other people prefer to leave a light on.

Meditation Exercise

- Sit comfortably in a chair with your hands resting in front of you.
- Close your eyes.
- Take a few deep breaths, letting your breathing slow down, and become steady.
- Let yourself be still and relaxed.
- Feel yourself become centralised as you put your thought process in a neutral gear.

- Think about what love means to you.
- Say a prayer, seeking help and guidance.
- Fill yourself with beautiful thoughts.
- Focus and hold onto those thoughts.
- As you breathe in, think about what you are actually breathing. The stuff you call air is a lifeforce, an energy that feeds the body. Thinking of it as energy will help you to see your breath as energy.
- As you breathe in, visualise the air and energy coming into you as a bright light, filling your whole body, revitalising you.
- See the light within expanding beyond your body.
- Let this light act as a coat or shield surrounding you.
- As you breathe out see irregular energy leaving you and going down deep into the Earth to be neutralised.
- Relax in the stillness of your thoughts, as you retreat into the inner sacred mosque.
- Spend a few moments with your eyes closed enjoying the inner stillness of yourself.
- Visualise yourself surrounded by a ball of energy and fill it with love and light.
- Once you have finished, slowly bring your focus of attention back to the physical reality.
- Move your fingers, wriggle your toes, gently move your head, feel the presence of your body.
- Open your eyes.
- Do not jump up and start rushing around in your daily activities.
- Give yourself a few minutes to be present where you are, once you have finished.
- Remember to give thanks and praise to God.

The first couple of times you meditate, you may feel a little fluttery in the stomach. It is usually because of the movement of your own spirit's energy, as it is cleansed and realigned.

To reflect in the mind is to enter a place within the inner self. Strive from there to see beyond your immediate thoughts about the worldly life. What you may hear and see in the mind is a reflection from the rivers of thought flowing through the land where you dwell. In this inner place, you have access to all you have ever experienced. The believer of untruths will love the untruth and hate the truth. The believer in truth will love the truth and strive against the untruths. With true belief, you can achieve whatever you will. As you meditate, you will see signs in your inner apartments. It is for you to learn the meaning of the signs and symbols. In meditation, focus on the light and allow it to guide you. Those of you who are steadfast will find they soon gather strength and determination in their new venture. Start with two sessions of *muraqabah* a day. One session in the morning and one in the evening, with an aim to increasing the length of time you spend at each session. As a guideline, the first sessions should last for about ten minutes at the start and end of your day. Build it up as a part of your daily practice. Use time only as a means, not an end. Start your meditation with a prayer of intention. God's helpers listen to your requests as you ask for help and guidance. Finish the meditation with a prayer, thanking and praising God. Meditation is something that takes practise. It is not a matter of sitting once and expecting something wondrous to happen.

If you enjoyed the first Meditation Exercise, be a little more adventurous with this next one.

Visualisation Meditation Exercise

- Close your eyes and let yourself relax.
- Say a prayer, seeking help and guidance.
- Visualise one of the following colours as a ball in front of your eyes or about six inches above your head.
- Red, orange, yellow, pink, green, blue, indigo, violet, white, or gold.

- If you have trouble visualising a colour, allow yourself to pretend. It will exist outside your inner vision.
- See the coloured ball of your choosing above or in front of you, draw it in or down, and let it enter your head.
- Visualise this colour moving down your neck, spreading out across your shoulders, moving down your arms to your fingertips.
- See the colour moving down your body filling you with its radiant light.
- Allow the colour to flow over your hips, down your legs, and out through the bottom of your feet.
- See this light going deep down into the Earth like the roots of a tree.
- Do this with each of the colours.
- Place into each colour the intention that your spiritual and physical bodies will be cleansed, balanced and healed from head to toe.
- Stay as long as you want in your inner world.
- Fill each moment with love.
- Surround yourself with a ball of light.
- As you come out of your meditation, slowly move your fingers, toes and head.
- Feel present in your body.
- Open your eyes.
- Do not jump up and start rushing around.
- Remember to return all thanks and glory to God.

If you find this does not work, try a different meditative approach until you find one that works for you. The different animals of the world move in different ways. They hop, skip, jump, roll, run, walk, scurry, crawl, wriggle, slither, float, swim and fly. If you were to draw a line between two points and place all the different animals at the start, eventually they would reach the finishing point according to their own method of approach. We all have a start and a finish. The pathway is the same for each person; only the approach makes it appear different.

Many people find the arts and leisure activities they do opens their heart in love. These activities act like a bridge between Earth and Heaven. Through their chosen activity, they raise their consciousness. It is the love for what they do that opens up the way. Inspiration is then able to flow into their consciousness. As they cross the bridge, it begins to unlock the door and into their minds is released an insight into their greatest potential. Music is the love of sound vibrations from which the musician produces a melody. Sound and melody are also the beautiful expression of the spiritual self in its address to other people. Dance is the love of movement. Everything in the universe moves to a rhythm. Drawing and painting is the love and appreciation of structure and colour. Everything in life has a structure of energy, sound and light. Each of us radiates with different colours, when our inner self expresses itself with love. Sculpture is the loving beauty seen in different forms. Without a structure, there can be no form. We must learn to appreciate the different customs and methods people use to achieve a oneness with God. God is a creative God and we must learn to see His expression in all activities and forms of life. If someone's outer approach to God is different from yours, it does not mean his or her approach is wrong. God will send to them exactly what they need to bring them safely home.

When you read the story from *The Quran* where God taught Adam the names of all things and the angels had no knowledge of such things. God was showing His angels the special favours he bestowed on humanity. It was made clear to the angels that God knows all secrets. That He knows what is revealed and what is concealed. Read *Sura 2 Verses 30-34.* Does God speak to other people in different ways, through different rituals and expressional activities and leaves you alone? God will establish a new people in your place if you refuse to take notice and listen. God speaks to you through the love you feel; no matter how you feel that love. Truly, God is the one who guides and not you. You will know what you need to know as a part of your inner self's development.

Sura 22 Verse 67
67. To every people have we appointed rites and ceremonies, which they must follow.

Through the expression of love, you will transform the three veils of darkness. To recap, the three veils that limit you are: certain types of thinking; overwhelming negative emotions; and a lack of willpower. During meditation, as you go within, create loving thoughts and listen to the loving wisdom that returns. Let your feelings take the place of your emotions. They will elevate you. From a position on high, you will see and accept many more possibilities about yourself. The realisation that you are much more than you think you are becomes a part of your understanding about yourself. You have to strive to overcome your fears and doubts as you expand or retract. You achieve this by looking within, seeing what is there, and repairing the damage done, the best remedy being love. Accepting responsibility must apply to all situations past and present. Forgiving alone does not take into consideration the blaming you may feel as you cast on other people your suspicions.

Sura 39 Verse 6
6. There is no God but He: then how are ye turned away from your true centre?

Many people turn away from their true centres. They are looking outwards for answers to inner questions in a bid to find a healing for their inner self. Put your trust in the inner voice as it speaks to you. When matters arise that cause you to create something other than love, do not embrace what arises. Instead, use self-restraint and recreate a new set of ideas for the story of your life. Your life does not have to have a disastrous ending. Repeat this inspirational affirmation in your daily practice.

Truths inside me rise and flourish
Like a flower in the sun.

Love spreads light through which I see
Heaven's door inside of me.

When we give an idea too much focus or attention, we deplete ourselves or add strength to the light. As long as the thinker is thinking about something, whatever the person creates gathers strength. The way to reduce the build-up of irregular thought is to cut off the supply. Irregularities soak up vital energy, not stopping until you stop feeding them. These thoughts will entwine themselves around you like a prison without bars. Do not let them reprogram you with thought programmes that darken your inner self. It is for you to interrupt and break the cycles. As you defuse the build-up of irregular thoughts, reach into the depths of yourself and sprinkle, like fairy dust, light on the darkness.

The thoughts of those who live at the furthest edges of their inner light can become an exaggerated extension of the truth. When you tell someone something, tell it without exaggerating or expanding the tale. The outer edge of the light is not where you want to be.

An exaggeration can have an adverse effect on the teller of the tale. Their mind creates a reality of conjecture that can be far from the truth. This will take you out of alignment with your inner truth. The truths that surround you are not complicated. They act as a guide or framework to hold you steady. Open yourself to them and they will disperse the wall of suspicion and separation. All truth expands from a central point. As you think and speak the truth, you will move towards the central light of your inner self. If you drift too far from your truth, it gently knocks at the door of your mind. It presents to you an opportunity, offering guidance back into the safety of its surroundings. Allow yourself to flow on the back of thoughts that take you to Heaven. If, during meditation, you find yourself drawn into an irregularity, acknowledge your position and say, "Thank you for your support, for you helped me on my journey". Be aware as you expand your inner-loving essence and climb up to the higher ground. God is indeed greater than the irregularity of your experience. Through His will, you are able to disperse all that is not of the light. Use this affirmation to help you on your journey.

I thank you for your loving care
As I express these thoughts that dare.
I seek to live on higher ground
Where love is shared all around.

When your focus of attention is in the direction of the material world, your thoughts, at times, appear harmless. This changes when you go within. When you close your eyes, you go into a world where your inner thought processes appear intensified. It is here that you begin to see their form. Measure their hold over you by the length of time you spend dwelling among them.

In *Sura 18 Verses 39-42,* there is a story about two men, each of whom had a beautiful garden. In the outer world, one may see something of the wealth of another. In the inner world, wealth hides from prying eyes. One of the men thought his garden was grander. In his hastiness to express this point to the other man, he allowed his tribal self to step forward. He gave the tribe a share in the handiwork of God. This caused a distortion and the garden of his inner self fell into ruin. You will find real wisdom shows up in the inner choices you make rather than in what you can present.

Your inner self is a garden of activity. Do you listen to God's will and truths as you enter your garden or do you choose to dwell among your weeds? Your irregularities can influence you into believing they have the answers to your life's questions. However, a little more digging will reveal all. The truth does not impose itself. Through your inner truth there is a suggestion planted within your mind. It suggests to you what you should do. The tribe arises to challenge the inspiration sent to you.

What does love really mean to you? Do you know what is contained deep within your loving feelings? If you do not express feelings of love, you will never know the delights contained. You are love. Love is strong. Love bridges gaps. Love heals. Love soothes. Love expands. Love knows. Love is taking responsibility. Love accepts responsibility. Love enhances your godly qualities. It is through the expression of your godly qualities that you become closer to God. Love is a beautiful spiritual condition. Love is God in action; love is the manifestation of spirit. Spirit is all things. In love, you find hope and through hope, you find the favourable winds that will carry you home. You can start by looking at the ninety-nine names of God and seeing how you can apply them to yourself.

Your growth depends on asking questions and listening to your inner truth. You must then put your trust in the truth; even if it goes against the conditioning you at one time accepted as true. Faith is a speck of wisdom that sits within you waiting to expand. Faith that remains undeveloped is so because there is too much doubt. Think about how you feel and why you feel this way. The thoughts you believe to be the truth may be no more than imposed conditionings from those around you. The: 'but this is what is expected', factor is not a good enough excuse. God's truth is clear, precise and simple, not arrogant or self-opinionated or filled with pride. Your perception about life is an accumulation of the thoughts you decided to accept as true.

All life moves to a rhythm. When you go against your flow, you get into difficulties. The art of knowing is to flow with truth and trust as you interact and experience what presents itself to you. Learn ways of working with all people in harmony; instead of demanding, ask what you can do for them. Learn to be of service. If someone comes to you flowing along a stream of energy that is distorted, you do not have to board their ship. Become the captain of your own ship and let love and wisdom fill the cargo hold.

Sura 16 Verse 111

111. One day every soul will come up struggling for itself.

You are your own key to opening the door that lets the information stored in the Heavens flourish in your life. Every one of us on Earth has to struggle for our own freedom by learning to expand our conscious awareness. As you clear away the irregularities, you reduce the mischief that plagues your mind. This will allow you to reside within those places on high.

God is always with you. If your inventions about God put Him in a small box at the other end of His creation, look within. You cannot rely on blind faith. Wisdom is available to you. Do you cast slanders about the hereafter from a position far off? Yet, *Sura 50 Verse 16* tells you that the afterlife is closer to you than your jugular vein. It is an irregular reality that makes the hereafter appear a great distance from you. Yet for those of you who are aware, it is a place so very close. People who believe God is not everywhere are expressing themselves according to their own limited awareness. They see themselves and all that is before them as separate from God. When you look within, you find that there is no separation between God and you. It would be impossible for us to exist in a place that God is not. God is the very sustenance that gives life.

The body is a vehicle for the spirit. You are borrowing this body. When you have finished with it, you will discard it and move on. The angels are nearer to you than your jugular vein and they reside in Heaven, which must be here and now. When you activate your feelings, elevating yourself in awareness, you realise Heaven is everywhere. Heaven is not up there, over there, or down there either. God is everywhere and everywhere is God. Love is the interconnecting energy. Love is the purest expression of spirit. There is also The Holy Spirit as mentioned in *The Quran*. This is looked at later.

All life is sacred and is on a journey back to God. For this journey to take place there must be a road that takes you there; a road that leads you to Heaven. How far you decide to travel along that road is up to you. Do not let other people influence you into thinking God has separated Himself from you. Do not see matter as a solid form and God as external to all forms. All matter is energy, and all energy is interconnected. If all that exists is energy vibrating and pulsating, how can there be separation between spirit and matter if one interacts with the other to create, give and sustain life? God sustains each one of us. For this to happen there must be an interaction between God and His creation. If you believe God is out there somewhere, separate from you, it is like saying your body and spiritual self does not need God to sustain them. One falsehood extends itself to another and the only other option that is left for you to believe in is that each of us is self-sustaining. Truly, there is an error in your thinking.

Sura 10 Verse 32
32. Such is God, your real cherisher and sustainer: apart from truth, what (remains) but error? How then are ye turned away?

Does your vision only look outwardly or do you turn it inwardly? When you look within, be sure you are turning your eyes in the direction of your inner light. The content of your thoughts will bring an instant recognition about your inner dwelling place. Your Guardian angels will speak words of loving truth to you in all matters concerning your spiritual journey. They know and understand the Spiritual Laws and will not interfere with your freewill choices. Through this freedom, you can volunteer to be of service or you can go your own way. Whichever you choose there will be an account held against you.

The word *Qibla* means the direction you face. Be among those of you turning inwardly in search of Heaven. The angels see and know those of you who have reached a point in their evolution to move on. The lessons of the physical world have balanced their three veils of their thinking, feeling and willpower. While in your home, your vision points in the direction of the world you wish to be a part of.

Those of you who turn for guidance in the direction of the sacred mosque, find the best of places to visit. To attract the angel's attention, use this affirmation.

Angels of light step into my life.
From my light to your light, I reach out in love.
From Heaven, I ask you to fill me with truth.
Perfecting my light and making it bright.

Sura 20 Verse 25
25. (Moses) said: O my Lord! Expand me my breast.

This verse describes a symbolic way Moses asked God to expand his awareness. As you lean towards the light, work to raise your consciousness through the degrees. As you travel along the pathway of light, inspiration about the land where you dwell is seen by you as thoughts and images in the mind. The best way to let your light expand is to surrender and ask for God's help and spend time in meditation.

If something has intelligence, there must be something with a greater intelligence behind that intelligent activity inspiring it on its journey. Science has managed to isolate a subatomic particle. This particle is smaller than a mustard seed, smaller than an atom. From this, scientists have evaluated that energy does not die. What the human eye sees when looking at the physical body is a collection of billions, or trillions, of tiny particles; each particle a life force. Each one influenced by your thoughts. The particles that make up your body have agreed to come together to help you. You can influence each particle, although you are not aware of this. Each particle chose to take on the pain and anguish you call experience or suffering to help you grow.

Sura 24 Verse 24 verse explains that our physical body holds within it information that will bring forth a truth about our actions in the physical world.

Sura 66 Verse 8
8. Our Lord! Perfect our light for us and grant us forgiveness: For thou hast power over all things.

The light that runs before you is the light that projects from your inner self. Those of you who meditate will seek and ask God, through prayer, to expand their breasts and perfect their light. They are the people who seek direct contact with those who can guide them according to the divine will of God. Be patient, yet labour hard. Strive to hold yourself steady. We are all here to learn lessons according to our spiritual needs. You cannot avoid these lessons because the lessons are a part of life.

Sura 41 Verse 30
30. The angels descend on them (from time to time): "Fear ye not!" (they suggest), "Nor grieve!"

As you raise your consciousness, you will feel the presence of the angels around you. You will feel the love they have for you. You will experience the truth of what awaits you in Heaven. You know what part of your inner self you need to work on and develop. As you look within, you will see sparks of illuminated light before you. The light of the Heavens will radiate out from you, ever changing as you change. As you look at the world, everything you see looks back at you with the same curiosity. The moment you try to possess the things you see they will seek their freedom in the same way you seek freedom. Accept that all things are in motion. Allow what flows into your life to flow out when it has served its purpose. Each time the things you have, have served their purpose they too become closer to God.

Sura 56 Verses 71-72
71. See ye the fire, which ye kindle?
72. Is it ye who grow the tree which feeds the fire, or do we grow it?

These verses are filled with inspiration and meaning. The green tree is metaphorical for the tree of life. Through this tree, you receive energy. The colour green is one of many colours used in the restoration of your inner self. Green is the symbolic colour of growth and regeneration leading to transformation. It is one of the colours of the heart centre. Green stimulates and develops growth towards true knowledge. It washes over you, cleansing you, realigning and reprogramming you with its essence. It brings with it, knowledge that sits within you, waiting for you to turn your consciousness within. As you enter its presence, it will reveal what is contained within itself. As you grow and develop, so too does the fire within you. The manifestation of loving energy from within gives the colour of your inner self its grandeur. Each colour you see has its own vibration and holds specific qualities to realign, restructure, heal and build the ships you use to sail the oceans.

In your meditations, you will see some of the lights join like clouds into a cluster. Rain symbolises the spiritual energy that washes over you, cleansing you. As the light comes together, there will be moments when the inner light you see is so bright, it is almost blinding to the inner eyes. It is not the light's brightness that causes you to flinch and turn away but its radiant beauty. Expressing love allows you to enter into the light without flinching. As it fills you, it will radiate around you. It will enrich the material world as well as yourself, cleansing you of base-matter energy.

Consistency, steadfastness, firmness and self-control are important for the journey. You could say that they are the tools of your trade that help you to complete your journey. Your job is to learn how to use them wisely and find your own way home. Love the life you are living, knowing all that happens is an opportunity for spiritual development and growth. Enjoy your life and take that happiness into your meditations. In happiness, you will find hope. In hope, you will find the strength, courage and a belief to continue. The light you bring back from your inner journey will help you and other people because it revitalises all it touches.

Sura 7 Verse 205
*205. And do thou (O reader!) bring thy Lord to remembrance in thy
(very) soul with humility and in reverence without loudness in
words....*

What is it without loudness of words? A thought is a silent word. As you go into your meditations remembering the name of God, let the energy and vibration from this remembrance fill you. Your growth depends on how you direct yourself. If you cannot interact with someone else in total love, then you have not heard the greater truth speaking. As you meditate, the light of your inner self will ascend like the rising of the sun. As your light shines, your irregularities will dwindle away. As you express love, you fill with love. You have to learn to direct your own self into the love and light of God.

Chapter 4: Self-Awareness

What you believe is impossible will show up within somebody else's awareness as a possibility.

The most important work you can do is on yourself. In this chapter, we will explore ideas about self-awareness, self-development and self-management. Before we do that let's have a look at an inspirational verse from *The Quran.*

Sura 47 Verse 31
31. And we shall try you until we test those among you who strive their utmost and persevere in patience: and we shall try your reported (mettle).

Meditation is a purpose-filled journey of awareness. You go on a journey into the depth of your inner self, a journey that takes you in the direction of the inner, sacred mosque. In this place, you become more consciously aware of yourself as a spiritual being in a physical body. You realise there is a part of you that is far greater than you can possibly imagine. It is in your sacred mosque that your wishes and dreams become real. As you go beyond the physical senses and connect to the more subtle spiritual energies, they bring to your mind revelations about a part of you that operates and works in other dimensions beyond this physical reality. You become aware that many of your worldly thoughts are but abstract aspects of yourself or energies of conjecture. As you stand between the physical and the spiritual worlds, the faculties of the spirit, body and brain give you the opportunity to experience different dimensions at the same time.

Your self-development is something that takes time and effort. Learn to work individually or as a group, allowing the light within you to expand. Create a harmonious atmosphere so you become one body of light. Work with patience and dedication knowing that you are not alone in your endeavours. Patience, firmness and steadfastness are the keys to success. Rewards will come from God in accordance with His will. Patience gives you calmness and clarity of thought when faced with difficult situations. Firmness balances you as you hold your concentration. Steadfastness enables you to push on without swerving. Through *muraqabah*, you start to free yourself from the wants and demands, the irregularities believe are important. You think; 'Why am I here in this world?' You are here to develop and expand your conscious awareness.

Many of your thoughts are programmes of events in the mind of the thinker. Therefore, it is good to take a step back and view what arises within from a distance. In your moments of stillness, among your thoughts will be heard truths. As you close your eyes and look within, your face turns in the direction of the Heavens. Work to hold yourself steady and flow with a favourable wind. As you do, you will get an opportunity to meet the angels who watch over you, each is ready to assist you on your journey.

If you have never explored your inner world, how will you know it is there? How will you know what is there? How can you develop and expand what you ignore? Refusing to listen is refusing to accept God's divine guidance and truth. Unless you visit this inner place, you will always be like a stranger in the sacred house of God, although it is walking with you all the time. The truth from this greater part of you becomes but a flicker of light in the darkness. The truths that you hear from within come to help you. Have respect for the light, truth and trust, acknowledging its entrance into your life. When you listen to the truth, you become a part of the truth. If you do not follow its course, how will you ever know the full answer to the questions that you seek?

You limit your awareness by restricting what you are prepared to know and understand about yourself. Through the listening to irregularities, many people's vision became blurred. As you listened to what was whispered there manifest within you, a partial truth. With the creation of this new land of thought activity within you, the more you listen to it the more it can grow. Then, you step forth into it. When this happens, the need to feed the spiritual self becomes a forgotten way of life. As you enter this new land, it creates a place within your conscious awareness whose thirst soaks up the sustenance sent by God to balance, heal and restore you.

Through inspiration, the angels say; 'Do not allow conjecture to be your guide. You have to learn to manage your thoughts. Self-management is how you organise and carry yourself on your journey. As you enter the manifested scenario, your constructed thoughts will create an outcome, before you even get to the end. The outcome will be according to how you decided to manage yourself during the experience. For you it becomes your plan of action but we see it as your self-management procedure'.

If you manage your time wrongly, you are always late. By taking responsibility for your time-management, you will always be on time. You could say, lateness is a lack of awareness of the importance of time in the physical reality.

Your awareness and understanding of your self-management procedures will help you. Self-awareness, self-development and self-management are good friends to have. Those of you who are organised and disciplined succeed because they have chosen to maintain and follow the best of truths.

You are not a failure because within you are unlimited potential. When you enter into a state of surrendering, you will defeat all self-sabotaging attitudes. You know that certain thoughts limit you but how many times in your life have you proven that by overriding such thoughts, using the wisdom of your evolved self, you can achieve. Why? You believed in the vision the wisdom presented to you. You opened your heart in love and the information contained within the seeds of wisdom revealed the truth. Your positive belief created the right light energy. The Law of Attraction then transported your consciousness to Heaven. The truth added to the light of your inner self, building light on light. This gave your vision a greater view, enabling you to see in a clearer light. The angels walk by your side and will inspire you, yet they will not take on your responsibilities.

Sura 5 Verse 46 makes you aware how every one of your thoughts, feelings and reasons, call them what you will, acts as laws by which you live your life. As you act according to your thoughts, you can see how the truth, the Spiritual Laws, your moral codes and conduct, interconnect. The greatest truth is contained within the light of your inner self. In the movement of the light and the darkness, truth reveals itself as one opposing force challenges another. Does it not make sense to look deeper within yourself to find the answers to your spiritual questions?

Throughout the ages, many books sent to enlighten humanity have helped in the process of awakening. They did not only appear, but entered into this world through people who expanded their consciousness and elevated their station. This knowledge, then becomes firmly grounded and anchored as it establishes itself in our hearts and minds.

As we each follow our own inner expressions of love, we will each eventually arrive at the same place, together, as one. For the same loving guidance speaks from a central point, in different ways, to all.

Work to expand what plants itself within the garden of your consciousness. As you implement your self-management procedures apply yourself in the direction of the light and you will cultivate your garden.

If you decide you want to turn away and travel to the outer edges of your inner light, the truth will follow you, always staying within your vision. No matter how far you travel in the land, the truth will always act as guidance to bring you safely home.

For each of us there are angels watching over us offering guidance. Where there is guidance there is always a governing law. The angel that is guiding does not escape the law. It must be aware of the divine plan by which it guides. Each of us has within a set of procedures that guide us as we travel. As we become more aware of the wisdom within, we experience a conscious shift. The first real signs of this are changes in our attitude.

Allow thoughts of inspiration to empower you. Develop the planted seeds of wisdom. Your overall self-development is what you recognise as learnt activity after the experience. The growth that takes place within you reveals your truth. It is the continuous cycle of the beginning and the end result because one is a platform for the other. As you strive and raise yourself up, what you currently dwell within eventually becomes a river beneath your feet.

Through self-awareness, self-development, self-management, and spiritual development you can bring success into your life. Go out into the world and seek what you enjoy doing. Do it as well as you can and you will always be successful and happy.

Self-awareness; Self-management; Self-development

1. Self-awareness is to be aware of the self and understand the workings of duality within yourself.

2. Self-management is how you express yourself as you implement your plan, after you have drawn on the light or darkness of duality.

3. Self-development is the expansion you feel and how you maintain yourself after you have implemented your plan.

Self-awareness is multi-dimensional and each person is able to expand in awareness in one way or the other. The individual may sometimes lose their vision and in a moment of hesitation, expand in a direction that leads to a state of confusion. Allow yourself to enter into a state of love. A noticeable transformation will take place within the awareness of your consciousness. Through transformation and change you see with greater vision.

Through inspiration, the angels say; 'Raise your consciousness through love, reach out to us. By doing so you will feel the benefits of knowing greater things. There will appear a light before you showing you the way. Through the light, you will feel our love as we join with you through the heart centre. As you work to disperse those self-contained programmes, those self-inflicted wounds, you will experience a greater state of calmness. Life is not about staying still or living in the past. Neither is it about dwelling within the cycles of thought that keep looping and cycling and chasing each other around, like the dog that chases after its own tail'. Throughout your life, you learn lessons, leading to awareness. Reach out and speak to your Guardian angels, they will reveal secrets to you by the leave of God.

Sura 30 Verse 30
30. No change (let there be) in the work (wrought) by God: that is the standard religion: but most among mankind understand not.

You are spirit. Your inner essence is spirit. Spirit is the pattern on which God has made each of us. Light is an expression of the condition of spirit. Those who purify their inner self become filled with a beautiful light. Work with the awareness of your spiritual self. Focus on reducing your irregularities. Work for God according to the patterning from which He has made you.

In life, every kind of possibility is presented to help us learn and allow us to expand our conscious awareness. In your moment of pondering, you will detect the possibility of a higher wisdom ready to help and guide you.

It is through your development and growth that you become aware of what you did not know. You only think something is impossible because you have not fully realised its existence. As you open your awareness, those things hidden, reveal themselves and the impossibility becomes the possible.

Raise your consciousness and you will come to know all things are possible. The people who make it to the centre of the garden where the impossible becomes the possible, have indeed worked hard. Work on your own relationship with yourself. Work with the inspirational truth God sends to you. Work with other people and work on your own evolution so you can make the transformations necessary to carry you consciously beyond the belief that something is impossible.

Through the inner light, you will find the guidance you need. Create the right conditions that will help you to detect new lands, where new growth awaits to expand and establish itself within you as a new possibility. For what you believe is an impossibility will show up within someone else's awareness as a possibility.

Our physical senses do not always tell us the full truth but presents to us something that is acceptable and believable. Our ability to think helps us to make a choice as we explore our emotions and feelings. Our moral codes of conduct help us to keep a balance between what is acceptable and what is not acceptable. If you wish to develop, you must bring your emotions under the influence of your feelings. Instead of acting on negative emotional impulses, allow your feelings to create and suggest thoughts to you. Your negative emotions can get in the way of your feelings in the same way your intellect can get in the way of your reasoning. An expression of loving feelings towards yourself creates a much greater feeling of love than a discharge of negative emotional apathy.

As you meditate, your inner vision becomes clear and you will marvel at your expanded view of life. You see what is unseen by many other people. Concentrate, directing your feelings towards the centre of what your vision beholds. Concentrate on expanding the light. By seeking a balance, or fine tuning yourself, you will reduce the negative emotional activity you experience. You will never fully realise how limited your emotional irregularities keep you until you have expanded your awareness.

Light of my inner self rise up within
Let me see you with the inner eyes.
Empowered, I stand in this centre of light
My heart do I open to give me insight.

Many people have had an experience of knowing something was going to happen beforehand. We use the words; "I had a feeling that was going to happen". Have you noticed we do not say; "I had an emotion that was going to happen?" Be aware that as you work with your feelings, there is a shift in your consciousness. You have stepped into a greater sacred space. Do not allow your irregularities to enter the equation or doubts will arise. Strive to change and follow the truth instead of what arises as doubt. The fact that you recognised the feeling tells you that you are ready to start learning. It is for you to pay attention to these moments of inspiration in your life. When what you felt comes true, do not allow the irregularities to suggest to you that it was a lucky guess, or chance occurrence. If you experience something once, you can experience it again. It may take you some practice to differentiate between what you are feeling. You experience your emotions in your stomach area, whereas your feelings are in your heart. Learn to use your emotions and your heart centre at the same time. Do not be a person who intertwines their truth with partial truths, as a means of giving certain experiences meaning.

The expression and expansion of your loving feelings takes away the control that self-sabotaging thoughts try to exert over you.

When your vision of perfection is not perfect, you believe that what God sends you in life is not perfect. If you do not agree with God's order in your life, it is but a lacking in awareness. Only when you believe all is perfect will you start to align yourself with perfection. We create our own version of perfection from the multitude of thought programmes and images we agree or disagree with. How can you see perfection if you are always complaining about its ordered sequence? Here is another affirmation to help you with this aspect of your self-development.

Within me is perfection; let it become a part of my vision.
Within my heart is wisdom to help me in my choice.
Within me trust and truth resides; let them be a part of my vision.
Within me there is light to help me see in perfect truth.

You may have a different cultural background, mannerisms and ways of doing things. However, this does not stop you thinking the same or having similar thoughts to someone else. Love is love, steadfastness is steadfastness, and patience and self-control have nothing to do with your worldly origins or nationality. A musician feels and goes with the flow of the music, producing melodies of inspiration. Different countries have different scales for their melodies but in the end, the result is a tune. Different musicians from different countries can come together and play their instruments in the style to which they are accustomed and produce a beautiful melody. Because of the different styles of music played, people who are musically aware will appreciate the melody to a greater degree. There are people who listen to the sound of their inner truth and appreciate it. There are people who listen to that same inspiration but do not hear the beauty to the same degree. God sends the same inner truth to each of us, to establish understanding and to guide us safely home.

Your perception of spirituality is according to your expression of love. Love does not confine itself to a particular group. There are people all over the world becoming more aware of their own true spiritual natures. Only love can produce a light, only light can shine bright enough to allow you to see the things hidden. Here is another affirmation for you to practise.

I am in you and you are in me.
The way I love myself is the way I will love you too.
All that I am, all that you are.
In our centre the same love, truth, trust and light.

You are the instrument. The melodies of love you express become the music of your spiritual self. The musicians who do not tune their instrument will not blend in with the rest of the players in the band. Examine your thinking when faced with an experience. To think something, you have to draw on the will of God. To feel something, you have to draw on the will of God. To exert motivation, you have to draw on the will of God. You draw from God according to your inner light. Nothing happens unless God wills it and all sustenance comes from God. He is the conductor of the band. He has arranged His instruments and their melodies in perfect order. Some will go out of tune and need retuning but they are always within God's melody. As He conducts, it is for you to pay attention. People who read and hear the musical melody, learning how to respond and conduct themselves as the conductor conducts, they will remain in the main band. The rest live in hope of one day joining the main band as they work to develop their melodies.

Nothing is ever wasted. Your supplies will reach you when the time is right. Have patience on your journey as your life unfolds. Do not paint a picture about what you think spirituality is. By feeling in the light of truth, you will learn to think in the light of truth. You will automatically direct yourself and enter the truth. Your thoughts within your loving feelings will show you the way to Heaven.

When you start to meditate, do not think you have to eliminate every thought. It is not so much a matter of eliminating every thought but of reducing their number. It is a matter of knowing what to listen to. It is for you to make a choice as to which thoughts you decide can board your ship. One small thought can contain all you need to know. Without thoughts, you will have no direction. Thoughts of love and truth contain a greater healing for you, so you need to construct fewer. Untruth or partial truths need extra thoughts to justify their existence. You will find that on the inner journey love is a beautiful expression. It does not need to justify or explain itself.

Chapter 5: The Law of Cause and Effect

According to the relationship that you have with what exists within your conscious, subconscious, and unconscious, the tribal self and evolved self, the result creates your reality. To know yourself, you must reflect in the mind. Your mind is the door to the Heavenly abodes. It can also be a door to the land of irregularity. To create the best reality, you must seek the higher wisdom. You may not change the people you attract, but you will draw out from people around you according to your own inner entertainment.

If asked; 'Who are you?' What would be your reply? Do you see yourself as the worldly labels and self-conditioning? You are unique. There is no one else like you. There is only one of you. In your development, if you feel you are not getting anywhere, examine the thoughts you create about yourself. You are a wondrous creation and within you is the potential to be a great human being.

You are a child of the universe whose journey has brought you to this world. You are here to halt your fall and return to the Heavens. You are here to develop your inner godly qualities and enter Heaven through the inner light. You are here to be a channel for the love of God. You are here to increase in awareness, the inner core essence of Adam and Eve. You are here to be of service. God is with you all the time. Go within and start a relationship with God. Doing so will change your feelings of belief into a full flame of bright beauty. You get to know God through the truth and the trust within yourself. God's love does not change but your awareness of God becomes ever deepening, ever expansive. God's love is something you can experience here and now. You cannot stop life expanding, changing or moving in a particular direction by trying to recreate the past. Everything on the face of planet Earth flows and fluctuates. You are a part of that fluctuating energy. If you do not flow and fluctuate along rivers of loving energy, you become ruffled and swerve from the path.

Sura 34 Verse 49
49. Say: The truth has arrived, and falsehood neither creates
anything new, nor restores anything.

The truth will restore your light. As order must follow chaos, falsehood must give way to truth, trust and change. There is nothing wrong with change. It is something that you do all the time. Listen to the small voice within and it will lead you through the changes you need to make. Your life, through the eyes of emotional logic, needs refining using your feelings and creativity. Eventually, wisdom presides as you learn how to construct your thoughts in a way that enlightens you. For people who wear glasses, think how different the world looks when they put them on; how clear and sharp the picture becomes. As you journey through life and you apply your feelings, they become a greater active force within you. As you listen to the evolved self and strive for change, the image before you comes into focus. The Spiritual Laws begin to stir in a new way, as they impress themselves on you.

In the reaping of what you have sown, do you set up a loop between one memory of an event and another? Do not add your imagined memory? As you cycle between the two, the conclusion traps you inside. During your lesson, do you become stuck, or do you transform yourself into light? If the image is born out of irregularities, there will appear on you a dark spot. If you follow its course, it will increase in size. Do you stare in bewilderment or are you happy it was born? You will cycle around and around until you forcibly shift your consciousness in another direction.

Learn to feel the difference between an inspired spiritually-related recall and a historically-related memory recall. One is inspired, whereas the other is based on your accepted historical belief of an event. Use your feelings and creativity. They see beyond the negative emotions that can block your inner vision. Step into a new grace and flow and listen to your feelings. They expand you to a greater awareness. Going within, seeing what is there and filling it with love will disperse and break down the cycle of historical conjecture. When in loving meditative prayer, each word, each sound builds light. The light breaks down the prison bars, allowing you to feel safe. Once you have let go of the thoughts that block your vision, your mind will clear and you will see true. New thought constructions from the light will present before you a new inner vision. Your goals will change as you strive to complete your life.

Break free of those recurring thought patterns that limit your ability to grow. Use a positive experience when you want to programme yourself to aspire. Use your memory to recall an event where you excelled. As you feel yourself stand in the centre of the moment, draw on your feelings and apply them to the task in hand. This is a great way to help you unlock your greatest potential when you need it. During meditation, you can create new images and transform that old memory into something new. These images will carry on working silently for you, breaking down, transforming and building a new platform of confidence on which you can stand.

Ponder on what part of your thinking and action is a conditioned response. Notice what thoughts or types of conversations you are always expressing when faced with certain situations. The best way to recognise your conditioned thought process is to watch your family, especially the children. They will mirror you and you will know exactly how powerful conditioned responses are. You have the freedom to believe, imagine and change. Be a child, free in the way you express yourself. It is up to you what thoughts you apply to the physical events manifesting around you. Thoughts give your perception of the world meaning, shape and form. Use this affirmation to develop these skills.

In myself are all the answers
To change, expand and grow.
Light energy reprograms thought
From within my heart, I am taught.

If God did not allow us to have an inner expression and manifestation, the outer activities around us would have no meaning. Your life is as real or unreal to you as your thoughts make it. What would you do if you had no memory, no thoughts in your mind? You would remain stationary. The accumulation of what is there creates your reality. If no thoughts exist, then you will have nothing to propel you into action. The life you live exists mainly because you think it so.

Let us say you go shopping. You first create an ordered sequence of thought activity. You set off on the journey and the shop is at the centre of the experience. On your way to your chosen shop, you pass by all the other shops until you reach the shop at the centre of your experience. Walking through its door, you enter that central reality. Once you have delighted yourself, you exit the shop, thus exiting the scenario. Your focus of attention then shifts to the next event you wish to experience.

The things you plan today, build tomorrow. Building the best future for yourself and your family starts with you and the happy, loving relationships you create. When you think about something, you give it life. You also become what you think. As you expand on your ideas, you will change your inner interior. Start by expressing love and construct pictures and images that work for you. In the transformation of your expression, your spirit's vibrational energy goes through changes. Expand your awareness and know. Seek the pathway; push through your thoughts of irregularity until you reach the light. As your consciousness resides within the light, you will feel its warmth on your face. You will feel its energy filling you and radiating around you.

The Quran speaks many times about not having any other god except God, yet the creation of irregular thoughts appear in the landscape of your mind. To maximise your meditation, pay no attention to the irregular mental images that come between you and God. You will find with God it is not what you ask for; it is through the expression of how you ask that provisions are granted you.

The following will help your dreams come a little closer. Get into the habit of meditating each night and morning. Allow yourself to bathe within the light. Once you reach the light, you will know what it is that will bring profit to you. Let the things you wish to manifest remain between you and God. Telling other people what you wish to manifest takes away its creative power. Do not leave your manifestations open to sabotage from other people.

Sura 24 Verse 25
25. On that day God will pay them back (all) their just dues, and they will realise that God is the (very) truth, that makes all things manifest.

Intention for Manifesting

Setting your intention aids the manifesting process. Be aware of the way you ask for the things you want. There is a well-known story about a fight that took place between two men during the early Islamic wars. As the non-Muslim was about to be slain, he spat in the Muslim's face. The Muslim who had the advantage in the struggle drew back because he became unsure about his motive for killing the man. Would it have been an act of war or was it because his opponent spat in his face? As he could not decide on the motive, he let him go. You too should have no doubts in your mind. If you want to make a change in your life, for example, a new job, making the following intentions is a way of preparing the garden before you plant the seeds.

Four Intentions

1. Nothing should be manifest that is not in accordance with the greater good of all.

2. Your intention should not be about doing a specific job at a specific place. All what is good for you will arrive in your life and be right for you. If you create as part of your intention that you should start work at a particular place doing a particular job, you set up the circumstances where someone else could lose their job. You should not wish to receive something 'like a thief in the night'. That is the power of intention followed by thought activity and visualisation. Also, be aware that what you create in error will not last.

3. We all need money to help fulfil our wishes and dreams. You need to think about this carefully and it needs to be in line with your needs and capabilities at the present moment. If your intentions are not realistic, centre yourself in your love, truth, trust and the light or you will create errors.

4. Be prepared to release the creation and let it work its magic for you and the greater good of all and remember to give thanks and praise to God.

Repeat this affirmation to help you.

I call on God and the truth and trust
To manifest for me.
The energy, sounds and light
To make my life complete.

You will come across wisdom as you prepare to create. It will tell you if what you are wishing to manifest will advance you or send you in a downwards spiral. Remember to keep your visions and surrounding thoughts simple and specific so you can re-enforce them by repetition in the following days.

Creating Through A Manifestation Meditation

- Meditate and surrender your whole self in love.

- With closed eyes, expand your awareness.
- Become aware of the spiritual presence within yourself.
- Recognise your unity with all things.
- You have now entered the inner light.
- Before you, you will plant the seeds of your dreams into your garden.
- Visualise the image you want.
- Encapsulate it into a seed casing and fill it with a pink light of love.
- The pink light will fertilise your seed.
- Fill your seed with the green light of growth.
- Place your seed into your garden.
- To release the energy of truth and trust, surrender yourself completely and express loving feelings.
- Send this energy into the seed.
- As you put your trust in God, hand over the whole scenario leaving the finer details to God.
- Give thanks and praise to God.

As you meditate, clear out any irregularities so love can freely flow through you without interruption. There are many sayings such as; 'Money is not everything' that self-sabotage you from bringing abundance into your life. Common sense tells you that money is not everything. Be humble in your needs. Money allows you to do the things you wish to do. Money is helpful but it is also an entrapment. Allow money to come into your life. Also, allow it to move on. When it moves on it leaves room for more.

You have one ultimate destination in life. How you make that journey is up to you. Do not swerve or be distracted until you have reached your true centre. Do you return with thoughts built from a foundation of the three veils of darkness and limitation or do you transcend these and return greater than you were?

As you travel into the greater states, you will hear whisperings from your irregularities. They are as beasts that scatter themselves through your land. If you turn your attention towards them, they establish themselves to become deep-rooted seeds planted in your inner garden. They will indeed disrupt the good things planted. As you drink your fill, at some time in your existence what you plant within will play itself out in your life. According to your consumption is according to the intensity and impression they will have on you.

The Spiritual Laws are not there to judge you. They have been set up to help you grow and expand as you co-create, with God, your destiny. As you ponder, pay attention. Recognise and acknowledge their presence. Have the laws set up a meeting that you are on your way to? Has something arrived in your life? Has something left your life? As the laws apply themselves to your life, you raise your consciousness or you destroy your own light by your own thoughts and actions. Is your Guardian angel trying to get you to pay attention? Notice their subtle guidance. Do you keep noticing a certain number, a certain bird, a feather keeps on appearing in strange places, or a word keeps jumping out at you in your everyday life? These are physical signs and symbols. Greater are those signs and symbols seen with the inner eyes.

God's love for you is perfect. Within His expression of love, an allowance gives you the freedom to create. God does not see right and wrong in the way you understand it. God says He will give you all your heart desires. He does this by granting you anything you wish. When you close your eyes in meditation, you enter your own inner world where you are free to create. As you reside within your garden, take care of it. After all, it is where you spend all your time.

What you send out from yourself comes back to you. The teachings that help you expand your awareness and raise your consciousness also help you to understand how best to work with the Spiritual Laws that surround you. For people who cannot comprehend the workings of the Spiritual Laws, they can but stare in despair as they pass through life.

Your stage of journeying must one day bring you to the place where the language within the Holy books reveals its wisdom. As you align yourself and follow the universal message, love being a key component, the Heavens will open. Do not rely on the outside world to satisfy all your needs. When you feel love, it is not something that is coming from the outside world of form, into you, it is something manifesting within you. Use the following affirmation to expand your own unconditional love.

Trust will lead me to truth.
Truth will lead me to the heart.
The heart will lead me to the light
The light will lead me to the place
Of unconditional love and grace.

The intellect is like one clock clarifying with another clock the existence of time. When you over develop your intellect, it can smother the truths of wisdom. The message the body creates via its impulses tells you that you will only find true happiness fulfilling its needs. The evolved self inspires you to search for the light of Heaven. We use our mind to reflect within ourselves so we may know the quality of our inner essence. By seeing what is within, we can clear and dissolve the blockages that limit our spiritual perception and awakening.

Whatever concept of perfection you have belongs to you. You may share similar views with another person in what you believe and say. However, you do not share the degrees of how much you feel about the things you share. Your spiritual perception formed out of your varying degrees of understanding, acceptance or rejection of a matter. No two people have the exact same view. This makes each of us unique. Other people have their own perceptions about life in the same way that you have yours. They have all the answers to all their own scenarios within themselves in the same way you have all the answers to your scenarios. When you do not immediately know the best answer, it is not that you do not know. You have to be still in the mind. Look beyond the energy blockage that clouds your vision and limits your conscious awareness. At times, your information will make you believe you have the absolute truth and the answers to everybody else's life experiences too. Your belief system will not be right for everyone even if you believe it to be so. The belief system you have is right for you. Accept the differences in other people and have a little compassion. Love is better than hate: compassion is better than judgement. You must discover the truths for yourself as to why the scenario or sequence of events before you came into existence. Through meditation and learning to focus, you can elevate your consciousness, placing it in a different degree or spiritual state of awareness. Within each state of awareness, there is a sacred mosque where you can meet God. You will find that what manifests through the eyes, filled with loving surrender, will bring about the greatest elevation in your consciousness.

Emotional love and feelings of love are quite different. Emotional love fills you with attachments to the physical world. Your feelings of love are free from attachments to the physical world. Your thoughts about certain patterns of loving activity will change as you move from the emotional to your feelings. Your interpretation about the meaning of the word love highlights the Law of Polarity in operation. We can end up doing all sorts of crazy things when emotional love manifests and expresses itself through us. You cannot blame another person and say; 'Someone else controls the way I think'. There is always something you can do to end the situation being played out in front of you. Someone may excite you into thinking in a particular way by playing out a scenario before you. However, the way you think and feel belongs to you. No matter what happens before you, you must take responsibility. You will find that the thoughts you attach to love rather than love itself, disorientates you. Take responsibility for entering the experience and playing your part. As you do, you will notice a change in how you feel about the situation. As you feel, listen to the new thoughts that arise because of your acceptance. Feel the calmness that washes over you. Put yourself in the other person's shoes. Exactly like you, they have their own matters of concern. Would you like the thoughts you have about other people directed at you? Remember that taking responsibility is different from taking or associating blame. Develop thoughts that are going to help you in life. If the skills you have are not working for you, change them. Much self-healing will take place in your life when you take responsibility for the manifestations that show up in your life.

Never allow yourself to be envious about another person's manifest experiences. Your envy will stop you from attaining in your own life. Envy manifests as a self-sabotaging destructive energy. If you hope things do not work out for him or her, your inner self accepts this as truth. The more it becomes a truth to you, the greater will its application apply itself in your life. Is your creative self then making a decision, saying; 'Therefore success or abundance must be a bad thing to create, so neither will it be created in your life?' You carry this around and it continues to play itself out in your life. If it should not be taking place for someone else, why should it be taking place for you? By wishing success on someone else, you will leave yourself open to success. The spiritual self lets you know that it sees and understands so it will recreate and add to you accordingly. The greater your happiness for other people, the greater and more successful you become yourself. You limit your awareness when you limit what you wish on other people. There is no limit to the amount of loving energy at your disposal in the manifestation of your dreams. There is an abundance to go around and it will not run out.

In the same way you pray and create, you then leave God to fill in the details. God creates in your life and leaves you to fill in certain details between the pre-destined landmarks during your time on Earth. God has arranged your destiny and its landmarks. You yourself have agreed to all you go through beforehand. *Sura 41 Verse 30* explains how God's angels do not interfere with your freewill choice but presents options for your consideration. Logic will never understand the divine flow of things. Life does not always follow logic and does not always fit into the small vision you have. God's plan for you is an ordered sequence of events in the larger game of life. Irregularities want to disrupt this divine flow. Teach yourself to accept matters on truth and trust. The light of your inner self is not there to trick you; it is there to help and guide you. Truth and trust are your true friend. Be patient. You want the cookies before you open the jar. The ordered sequence is to open the jar, look inside before taking out and eating the cookies.

Life can be like a game of chess. In the beginning, you may make a few strange moves, which confuses your opponent, however, you have a plan. At times, your opponent may see your plan and counteract the movements to disrupt your game. As you continue, certain moves become clearer as you and your opponent move pieces around the board. As you look at the pieces on the board, you have to put yourself in your opponent's place, working out what moves they are planning. Your opponent will never fully know your game plan. Right up until checkmate, you and your opponent will be in a state of pondering about each other's moves. Some of your moves will be in sacrifice, others in defence, whereas others will be in the direct pursuit of your goal. In the game of life, when you surrender yourself, you give yourself an advantage. You are still a player in the game. However, your strategy is but a different approach. Meditation puts you more in the game than out of the game. You can meditate anywhere. All the while, you and everyone else is pursuing their journey back to God. You may not know your opponent's game plan, but God does. He is behind all strategies, plans and movements and knows what you do not.

Where you are going will be there when you arrive, so sit back and enjoy the journey. Could it be that the meeting you cannot be bothered to attend will lead to a great opportunity for you? How many times have you been somewhere and the last thing you expected to turn up in your life actually manifests? As your life unfolds, what you call coincidences are pointers and indicators to help you on your journey. It is for you to learn to appreciate all that manifests in your life. Those things that upset you and those things that make you happy are manifestations you have agreed. Because you have not arranged them through your conscious mind, it does not mean you have not arranged them as an experience on another level.

Sura 7 Verse 56
56. Do no mischief on the Earth, after it hath been set in order.

Surrender and expand your loving feelings. As you follow through, a door to the Heavens will open and you will enter. The more of Heaven you let flow through you the greater becomes your spiritual abundance in the expression of godly qualities. You are entitled to many things through The Law of Abundance. You are the one who must cherish your godly qualities within. As they grow, they radiate love and light around you. It is through this love and light that you unlock the doors within yourself, welcoming Heaven into your life. There will be a time in your existence when Heaven's door of awareness opens permanently.

Do not believe you are the body more than spirit or you will not transcend its influence over you. See yourself in this world in the same way you see yourself in your dreams. Everything that manifests in your dreams has a message created by your inner self to help you grow and develop. Your dream experience was created through the greater part of yourself. Likewise, manifestations in this world are a part of, and are symbolic to your development. Through your greater self, you have a direct connection to God. This connection is the pathway along which you must travel. You receive guidance and inspiration through the evolved self as you manifest and co-create, with God, your spiritual journey.

Chapter 6: The Ship For Sailing

Sura 17 Verse 66
66. Your Lord is He that maketh the ship go smoothly for you through the sea, in order that ye may seek of His bounty.

God's bounty is within you. When in meditation, you are the ship sailing through the great spiritual oceans of activity. Seek to reach the station of Abraham, which is a state of consciousness where you will find security. However, before you reach this place of safety, you come across irregularities and they surround and fill you with doubts. They have no power over you except what you give to them yourself. It is for you to hold yourself steady and push on through until you leave them far behind. Also, read *Sura 10 Verses 22-23* because the meaning in these verses will help you.

Your thoughts are the sails of your ship. During meditation, as you reach out with your consciousness, you are like a ship sailing through the oceans of the Heavens. Through your thinking, feelings and willpower, you direct yourself. Unity is an important quality of any spiritual development. Your thinking, feelings and willpower need experiences to balance them. According to the direction and focus of your vision, the three veils meet at the same place. On your travels, focus your attention on the light. The practice of *muraqabah* will help you bring together the qualities necessary to build a vessel that will carry you. As you live your life, in your reflections about matters, you see before you the bridge of choice. *Muraqabah* lets you stand on the bridge; the dividing line that balances you between Earth and Heaven. How far you travel along the bridge depends on the love within you. As you enter the open spaces, watch for the signs of God. You have the ability to rise out of the lower depths and into the light. When you have built your ship with enough particles of light, you join with others who sail firmly on the sea.

People who practice *muraqabah* know there are times when they enter a place where they fully immerse themselves within the greater states of awareness. The sacred mosque you build is from your own love, piety, gratitude, truth and trust. The closer you get to God the more of His light will you find within yourself. Your understanding about God will change as you meditate and absorb His light.

You can see an example of this in the way communities have changed. In many shops, the introduction of different good and services you can buy has changed over the decades. As we intermingle, we adopt customs from other cultures. Your lifestyle, dietary and clothing changes as you absorb the different customs of the people who now live in your neighbourhood. In this same way, your awareness changes as you accept something new into your consciousness. As you express love and get closer to God, you pay more attention to His wisdom, inspiration, love, trust and truth as it comes to you through the inner light. Fill yourself with love and its content will become a part of your conscious awareness.

When in your sacred mosque, devotion to the service of God and humanity is at its peak. Yet, when you return to the world, you soon reconsider your promise. You will cry to God many times; 'Save me from myself, save me from drowning.' He will save you from drowning many times. He will do this until you can sail smoothly on the sea.

Steadfastness, firmness and patience are the keys to success. During your meditations, everything is fine. You feel nothing can stop you. You have a smile on your face and joy in your heart. The mind is clear, the eyes of your inner self see and your feelings sense before you the way to cross over into new pastures. In the coming days, you may ask yourself; 'Why am I now facing all these internal difficulties?' The reply will be; 'Your thinking and feelings need to develop, so too does the mental faculty of concentration. You have to transform the three veils of darkness. Hold your concentration steady without it wavering'. At some point, you will have to travel through the valley of the shadows in your final release from the trappings of this physical world. Would you go into battle without your armour? How long do you think you would last? The only way to survive the onslaught of forces against you is for you to become as strong as iron and keep control of your focus of attention. Reading *Sura 47 Verse* 31 will help you. Your strength and determination of mind is indeed tested.

Refuse to give up, yet always keep a calm repose. You may find yourself distracted by all kinds of thoughts. The past may plague you. The future may look uncertain. The present may worry you. If you are distracted at all, wait, for a moment. It takes time to build up the necessary strength. If you had nothing to strive for, you would become restless and look for something that tested you. Reason is the light of the intellect. Through the light, God and His angels will inspire you in your endeavours. Through listening to their suggested wisdom, you will find the answers you need to carry you on your journey.

Sura 3 Verse 153
153. Behold! ye were climbing up the high ground, without even casting a side glance at anyone.

Each of us goes through happy and sad experiences. According to our perception, we either add strength to our light or cause it to become dim. You are an accumulation of all that is; you are right here, right now, right where you are supposed to be. God is perfect. There can be no imperfection in perfection. All that happens to you is in line with perfection. Hold steady in the direction of the light and do not allow stray thoughts to distract you from the path. Hold onto the loving feelings and the light, hold onto the trust and truth, and you will not go wrong.

In limitation, you give a share of all that happens to the tribal self, believing it to be the creator of your success. Although we play a part in the co-creation of our own destiny, God has the final say in all matters. It is in this that the success you feel belongs to God because all matters go back to Him for a decision.

Sura 11 Verse 123
123. To God do belong the unseen (secrets) of the Heavens and the Earth, and to Him goeth back every affair (for decision).

As you develop and expand your awareness, your ideas about your reality change. As you raise your consciousness, you are able to command how the laws manifest in your life. However, for the majority of people, the laws command recompense. The Spiritual Laws manifest and then you choose which pathway you go down. Each pathway has its own experiences and choices that come with it. The laws are forever influencing and impressing on you in different ways. The laws work for you and with you or you fall out of favour with them. When they work for you, you are aware of the materialisation and dematerialisation process that brings creation together, giving it a beginning and an end. You are almost free from the bonds of the world and know, as you think, so shall it be. When filled with light, the Spiritual Laws obey your conscious thought. When they work with you, you are aware of the manifesting process. This place exists between the two points of polarity, between the beginning and the end. When you fall out of favour with the Spiritual Laws, your perception narrows down and all you see before you is action and reaction. What you perceive influences you and you become unsure of the end, so you hastily push and shove to try to produce outcomes you believe are desirable. In all matters, you will reap according to your actions.

On the inner journey, as you approach your true centre, you become aware of how the laws are working for you. Meditation and the manifestation of love and light will be a central focus in your life. When you are aware of the laws working with you, then meditation and prayer are central to your progress. When you are not aware, prayer, action and reaction become central to you. In all circumstances, your throne is central to all that is taking place around you. Around each of your actions or reactions, all things revolve. Use this affirmation to help you evolve.

Let myself on the ocean
Like a boat sailing, be bright.
Let myself on the ocean
Transform the darkness into light.

For a few days, you might struggle to control your consciousness, as you are tossed about by the storm. You will gain great spiritual strength as you plough the waves. It is you passing through your own storm. You have to battle against the self-sabotaging forces. Every time you enter, learn which expressions help you to control the direction you find yourself sailing. To fight in the way of God, it does not always mean a physical fight. There is a battle between the polarity of your inner self, where your feelings of love and a determination of will, must hold you in the light. You will not find peace in a physical fight because both parties receive wounds within. The Law of Cause and Effect will bring you back together, giving each of you an opportunity to heal the pain each caused the other. Read *Sura 2 Verse 20* to understand your times of help and struggle.

When you board your ship, you occupy a small space in the great scheme of things. The Heavens are endless in their depth, breadth and width. When the ocean of irregularity swells up, overwhelming you, you experience its trappings as it surrounds you, constraining you, yet beyond, Heaven awaits. Each degree of light is a Heaven, which is home to the people who dwell there. However, you should only be a passer-by until you can be sure you have secured your home in the highest horizon. Reach out to the station of Abraham. Look beyond what is directly in front of you. The storm that ruffled the surface will become calm by your command. You will find that beyond duality there is a sea that is tranquil and still.

Sura 37 Verse 10
10. Except such as snatch away something by stealth and they are pursued by a flaming fire of piercing brightness.

Sura 48 Verse 29, The marks on you are not necessarily the physical marks some would say are a result of the way that Muslims pray. *Sura 7 Verses 46-48,* People who have developed their spiritual vision will know and see these marks for they are of a spiritual nature. There is an inner prostration of humbleness and gratitude. In the future, among the enlightened ones, relationships will be according to these spiritual marks. They will be seen within the aura. It will be known, who is spiritually connected to whom. Among the enlightened ones, relationships will be based on spiritual compatibility. By now, you should be realising that there is a new world you have yet to explore. Humble yourself, it will reveal itself to you. Humility is not about being humble in your gestures to all the people you meet and at the same time mischievous and violent in your thoughts. There is a prostration, which takes place within. You must be humble before God and all life forms. The way back to God is through loving thoughts, words and deeds. Your inner self's light is an accumulation of energy, you yourself gained through loving thoughts and good deeds. Have you ever heard a story or known anybody who resides within the greater Heavens and they are filled with arrogance, anger, hatred, violence and has speech that expresses profanity?

The entrance to heaven is through the door of love. You enter the centre of your own light, standing as it were, in your own creation. What you receive as inspiration grounds you in truth as you explore beyond irregular thought patterns and images. In love, you send forth your prayers, wishes, hopes and dreams and they ascend up to the Heavens like a blade of grass breaking out of the Earth. The light surrounds your light and falls back on the sender adding more light to their inner self's light. The light makes you strong in readiness for when you take to the sea and sail with a favourable wind.

Once awareness settles down and becomes an organised foundation on which you stand, you will feel secure. You are among the many people who have through personal experience received proof and evidence of the life hereafter. The love you feel and the light you see during meditation holds the healing power of God. You are able to distribute it to people in need. You become independent and free from the doubting ones. Irregularities cannot remain in the greater realms of light. A piercing flame of bright beauty chases them. However, the light of love and inspiration easily finds its way into the conscious self in a hope that you are listening. As you draw on the light, it expands all around you, dispersing and transforming the irregularities. Every particle of light that falls on you helps in the building of the ship that you use to travel on the sea. People who do not build their ship from particles of light will find it difficult to remain in the light of Heaven. In the presence of the light, you live beyond the reach of the people who live in darkness. It is for you to clothe, with skill what you know so other people may partake. Those who refuse to listen to what flows through their evolved self can only rant and rave, but your light will protect you from the winds that they send forth.

What you do in the inner world is much more important than what you believe you achieve in the outer world. Hold on to the truth. In the hereafter, each of you will return to the place on which you built your foundation.

God is the producer of seeds and you are the sower of good deeds as the information in the seeds reveals secrets to you. Expand in love and you will experience the wonders and delights that the hereafter has to offer you. Take to the ocean in your ship. Sail through the seas in search of your home. Only through a commitment to change will you reach a land of pleasant surroundings. See the place within as your future home and visit it as often as you can. The qualities of God exist in different stages of development, from individual to individual. Let us all work together to bring out the best within each other.

Sura 13 Verse 14
14. For the prayer of those without faith is nothing but (futile) wandering (in the mind).

Your prayers attract the attention of God. Turn your focus in the direction of your true centre. Your true centre is your inner sacred mosque. If you do not create the right intention, your prayer will not pass beyond your lips. Words alone will not carry your prayers to Heaven where the angels embrace them. Spend time putting yourself in the right frame of mind. Your approach must be one of loving surrender. Activate your feelings around the words you speak. Take your time in your mind and be in the present moment. It is love that will carry your prayers beyond the reach of irregularities. When you pray or meditate and your mind wanders onto something other than establishing a conversation with God, it is as though you have stretched forth your hands and touched nothing. What is in your mind becomes the target of your prayers. Focus on a point beyond the irregularities in the mind. Those who do not surrender themselves will not enter the places you enter at the beginning and end of the day, especially if you are a person who meditates.

People who find they are spending time on their own, enjoy your journey. Being alone can be good for you. It gives you the opportunity to be yourself. It gives you a chance to invent ways of creatively occupying your time. If you are a shy person, do not believe that there is a lacking in who you are. Recognise that you are maturing in a different way to other people. As you unfold, you will find your place in life. Because of your maturity in spirit, your appetite for external things does not outweigh the balance between your light and darkness.

The shy person may find it can become a struggle coping with the behaviours of other people around them. See your shyness as a cloak of protection from God. It is a great blessing, however, you must learn how to work with it. If you brush your shyness off to follow other people in their ways, you will lose something of real value. As a child standing at the crossroads of life, you feel suspended between the material and the spiritual worlds. For people whose leaning in the mind is more in favour of the material world, it is easy for them to identify with what it has to offer. They have direct access to worldly activities. It falls into line with their perception and awareness, confirming and fulfilling their desires. These people go straight into its activities because they are not aware of anything else. They are as strange to you as you are to them. Most of the things you learn from other people, directs you to the fulfilment of the Earthly life. You can see the world, touch it and interact with it. Most of the things your enquiring mind encounters, you accept the answers from your peers whether they be a truth or partial truth.

However, what happens when you have those questions that no one around you can answer? Most of the things taught to you direct you to the fulfilment of the Earthly life. No one explains to you the things that will satisfy your inner yearning. You know that your immediate surroundings do not satisfy your needs. You see, hear and know events before they happen. You see or sense people who are not always there. You may have a special friend who visits you. At night, you might fall so deeply asleep that you do not fully register the needs of your body. Indeed, a matter, which is frowned on. You might dream about walking and talking with the angels. Now your questions become unacceptable. Your peers ignore you because the people you ask did not know the answers.

When you are young and growing up in the world, you are dependent on information from other people. Heavenly questions are beyond the comprehension and outside the scope of many people's vision, so you too place a cover over your eyes and ears and this inner world disappears for a while. This is when your cloak of protection is useful because it keeps you safe. Enshrouded in its mystery, you enter into the world and its activities until a future time.

Let your shyness take its natural course. You cannot live other people's life for them and they cannot live your life for you. Shyness keeps you safe on your journey. It keeps you in the real world. It sustains you from slipping into a world from which it can be difficult to escape. You will soon recognise those of you who are real from those who are lost. Your life will flow according to the needs of your inner self, not the fleeting desires manifested by certain individuals around you, so enjoy your journey. As you start to awaken and become aware, you venture out and explore new lands and new worlds. You are not so sleepy now, are you?

You should not be ashamed of your shyness. Work with it until you reach a time in your life when you are ready to acquire knowledge about the Heavenly life. This mysterious force enshrouds you, protecting you, enabling you to climb to a place where you see new horizons before you. Throwing away your shyness will bring discomfort to you. What you thought was low self-esteem will transform into self-confidence. You will be able to access and control the flow of light that comes to you. From there, you will easily gain mastery over the thoughts that caused you mischief in the mind. No longer will you be an orphan in the wilderness of life. You will blossom like a radiant flower, expanding your inner fragrance. You will meet again those from your childhood days, rekindling the love between you. You will enter the light and the angels will teach you how to permanently bridge the gap between Earth and Heaven. If you try to become anything other than the light you are, your revelation of truth will start to distort like a mirage. Unkind words will return when you retreat into the inner world, forming a barrier through which light would have otherwise radiated. These irregular thoughts are but created shadows swimming within. If you choose to fight against the protection that surrounds you, you have your freewill. You will find sustaining yourself from slipping down the degrees of light is a delicate matter. However, nothing is ever lost because on your way back to your Heavenly abode, you will gain wisdom. Through meditation and prayer, you will re-establish your awareness.

Good deeds and charity are good ways to produce benefits for you and your account with God. If you feel someone has done you a wrong, let it go. Give it as an act of charity, for God rewards those who give in charity. Hold onto the idea that God gives and He takes, to teach us not to grieve.

Thoughts play an important part in your development. Without them, you would be motionless on the ocean with nothing to drive you along. When you realise the truth about thoughts and their activity, you will take more care about what you think. Learn to hold yourself steady by creating thoughts that you know will expand your awareness. Ensure your prayers contain enough loving feelings to sustain them on their journey. A good way to pray is to listen to your thoughts of prayer and bring the sound of your voice into unison. Some of the stamps for your prayers are love, trust, truth, honesty, sincerity, gratitude, humbleness and surrender. These qualities raise your prayer to Heaven. The expressions of pure thoughts mount up to the Heavens because love carries them there. The replies to your prayer enter your inner garden. Love will open the door to the garden where you will find the seeds of Heavenly truth, from which you can extract your answer.

Chapter 7: The Law of Attraction

Read *Sura 13 Verse 41; Sura 6 Verse 125;* and *Sura 21 Verse 44* while you explore this chapter.

Do not rely too much on the physical body, believing its senses to be your only source of information and strength. Unless you work to expand your breast, symbolising the expansion of your awareness, you may remain confined and constricted to a world of limitation.

The internal lands you visit or reside in are temporary places where you sit, stand, walk, talk, eat and sleep. People who strive and are observant will be familiar with various stages of consciousness as they move around their polarity. We are all seeking to reside within the land where the sun forever shines. This land is through the light, in the highest part of our horizon. It is your task to remove yourself far from the tribal self, which has slain many people. This tribal self has swollen, holding captive many prisoners.

Sura 2 Verse 17
17. Their similitude is that of a man who kindled a fire.

Consider the flame of the candle, it burns brightly. The flame that burns within you is light. From a little light, you kindle it into a full flame of bright beauty. You know the irregularities will try to extinguish the light. You also know that the light will win over the irregularities. The best fires are the ones that burn brightly, fuelled by the light of love. If you cherish the seeds of light within, from a little light that flickers, it will become a flame full of beauty, radiating all around you.

To make something pure, you need to remove what is impure. In you, it is recognising the base matter into which you are born. From within this place falsehoods spring up. Self-restraint will help you to overcome the irregularities that manifest. Why will there not be the same kind of help for the unkind seeker in the same way there will be help for the kind people who seek? Firstly, the unkind seeker will have to create within themselves the right kind of weather conditions that allows their ship to sail smoothly. People who kindle the fire, drawing on the light, will pass into that light. In the darkness, they will not know of their helper unless they show signs of awakening. Around each seeker manifests a perfect order to help them grow and develop. Laws that reflect the perfect order govern all things. For you to recognise and flow along with the light of life, you must work to harmonise yourself with that perfect order. You must sail your ship along the rivers of love. Sailing against the flow, you will be overwhelmed.

Sura 77 Verse 8
8. Then when the stars become dim;

Sura 81 Verse 2
2. When the stars fall losing their lustre;

When travelling the path back to God, you will reach a point where you have received your share of proof and evidence. If you turn away, you will wander helplessly. The land that was once within your reach will be nothing more than a vague memory among clattering thoughts. You will have to unravel what you have woven. Listening to uplifting words will turn your garden back into a beautiful land. From the seeds of Heaven will grow fruits. Truly, as people who corrupt themselves, their light becomes dim. Read *Sura 24 Verse 55* and use the affirmation below to help you deepen your experience.

The land, which I am striving to reside in
Is but a place of rest.
Beyond the reach of those that falls
Where I can hear the angel's call.

Highly-evolved beings monitor all power and energy released into the land. From it, each of us borrows only what we need. As you develop, you will start to detect different vibrations of energy around you. Gradually, degree by degree, love builds up your inner light.

As you direct and hold yourself with consistency, in the direction of Heaven, you will pass into the greater states of awareness. The prophets came to Earth to teach us how we too can raise our consciousness. They demonstrated the true potential within each one of us. As we are all spiritual beings, what is within the prophets is also within each person in an undeveloped form.

People who believe must unite instead of blowing puffs of smoke at each other. Know that the truth is in all the religious teachings of the world. Certain people in different groups would have you believe otherwise, so it is best to ignore them. Do not look only at the surface of things. People who are unsure make but a show about what they think is with them. The rich person knows they are rich. The poor person is unsure about their wealth. During *muraqabah* you can enter the light and dwell within its open spaces. In your inner world, all people who dwell there are equal.

Irregularities cause many people to forget where their true home is. As you reflect within the mind, images of the land you will inherit impress themselves on you. You have spent all your life creating and preparing this land. People who take care of their garden will enjoy the land they inherit. People who strive, expressing love, will live in a spacious land of love. People who do not look after themselves will find that their light loses its lustre, becoming dim like the greyness of night. The thoughts that arise within are a good indicator as to the condition of the land where you dwell.

Sura 81 Verse 7
7. When the souls are sorted out, (being joined, like with like);

Sura 78 Verse 21
21. Truly Hell is as a place of ambush;

Indeed, it is a sad matter in the case of any who follow their own agenda born out of self-desires. The above verses explain the Spiritual Law of Attraction. In the afterlife, groups of individuals are joined in harmony according to their inner expression. The Spiritual Law of Attraction works on the principle that you attract or are attracted to, according to the content of your inner self. Be aware that your outer movements are only a small part of the inner state. The real you, hides from those who do not have eyes to see. It does not matter what you think your position is or what you present to people you know. You cannot escape the divine Spiritual Law of Attraction. This Spiritual Law will carry you to a place according to your inner expression. You will not gain automatic entry to the highest of Heavens by saying; 'I believe'. Neither will all your desires manifest in the way you want so you can indulge yourself. In the hereafter, love IS.

Sura 56 Verse 7
7. And ye shall be sorted out into three classes.

On passing from the physical world, some people become isolated from the rest, locked in a reoccurring scenario. Other people may also be with you, joined in harmonic accordance. There is no way of quickly changing your state once you take your leave of the physical world. It is much easier to do it while you have freewill and a physical body.

Expressing love attracts the attention of the angels who radiate love and light. Acts of self-restraint will sweep aside the fog of illusion. This will allow a stronger foundation of unconditional love to establish itself within you. Your acts of self-restraint will help you overcome past mistakes and old habits. As you shed light on your irregularities, the angel of death that dwells there will transform into light. When you throw away your true belief to follow in the ways of other people, it is a crime against yourself. You allow this infiltration to take place, which is a form of possession. Those of you, who twist the truth that comes to them, attract an entity likened to their twist. Truly, Hell is for some people a place of ambush because they chase what they hear from the base matter into which you are born. Strive forward and put your trust in God. What is waiting, will be better than what you left.

Read *Sura 72 Verses 18-19* and consider that there are people who wish to take your light. You may not see them but they see you. Some of the irregular thoughts you think, create or attract around you a dense crowd of people who try to stop you from entering the inner sacred mosque. Irregularities are not light and bright, but a swirling grey. You have to ask yourself and then decide, is what comes from yourself expressed in a loving way? Alternatively, is it flowing with feelings and creativity? If you have chosen correctly, as you set out on your journey and strive to climb the mountain, you will gain a greater view.

The body receives much nourishment from the thoughts you produce. The energy you draw in and around yourself travels through a network of energy vortexes called chakras. We discuss these towards the end of the book. Your thoughts affect every particle of your body as they lay down their patterning within you. Filling the body through the visualisation of love and light is the best way of feeding yourself with food from Heaven. Many people think; 'If God loves us so much why does He punish us?' Are you sure God is the one who punishes you? Do we punish ourselves? God has so much love for each of us that He allows us to inhabit a physical body so we may learn and expand our spiritual awareness. There is so much love for you that when you take your leave of this world, you are welcomed back to the hereafter with great joy. The love that flows through you in this world, flows through you in greater abundance in the next. You cannot blame God for the direction you lean in the mind. Have you accepted a life plan built on the sand cliffs? Has no one taught you the real meaning of love? You strive to acquire things out of your reach yet God is ever around you. God did not turn His attention away from you. Have you rejected the inner wisdom that came to you? When you turned your attention from your true centre of light, you forgot about the workings in your life of the Spiritual Laws. They continue to impress on you and are working with you right now. The inner expression of love will awaken you about how best to work with the laws. Many people give of the material things yet when it comes to the giving of love, they act so sparingly with it. Do not let material things be a substitute for your love. Within each person there are godly qualities waiting to express themselves. Their expression produces actions of good conduct that helps to build your light. When you surrender in love, the five pillars of Islam fortify the foundations of your life.

The Five Pillars of Islam

1. *Shahada*: the declaration of faith that there is no God but Allah and Muhammad is His messenger.

2. *Salaat*: prayers 5 times a day.

3. *Zakaat*: giving 2.5% of your wealth to charity.

4. *Ramadam*; a month of fasting - no food or drinks - during daylight hours.

5. *Hajj;* a journey or pilgrimage to a specific Holy place, Mecca.

Expressing love is the will of God in action. Expressing love is something that should flow from you. When you hold on to your love, it eventually clogs up with stale thoughts. When you give it out, you allow this energy to become an active force. There is nothing in the world you can substitute for the love you can give to someone else, from yourself. The love you give is the love you receive from God as your consciousness reaches out and enters the unlimited abundance that never runs out. Open yourself up to The Law of Abundance. Work to change the content of your inner self. Make a promise to yourself and for the next half hour, be in a state of love to all. No matter who you meet or what arises within, focus on expressing loving feelings. Do not say a harsh word to anyone and cancel out any irregular thoughts that arise. Extend this to a full day and be aware how your whole outlook on life changes. God's love knows no boundaries. When you step on this pathway, it shows that you believe in the divine plan you agreed, with God, to follow. Use this affirmation to help you express love, every day.

I open my heart so love can flow free.
I open my heart so I can see.
I open my heart; may God's love enter me.
I open my heart so love can be me.

Each of us has come to this world on a divine mission. The love you have agreed to work with is with you. Slow down in your pursuits for a while, instead of rushing. The right choices are contained in a few simple thoughts that lie within you waiting to be recognised. Seek for people who share a common interest in the way you feel. Get to know the land where you live. When you feel the presence of irregularities, there are loving thoughts that tell you to pull yourself together and you can make it through. Be there with these thoughts and follow them to a land of safety. Every moment of your life is a development process to enhance your awareness. During meditation, turn around your moments of struggle. It is a chance to develop and enhance the quality of your thinking, feeling and willpower as you sail on the seas of life. Let the truth rise and it will resurrect you, dispersing the heavy loads you carry. Each degree of light you pass through is a resurrection for yourself. What happens when truth arrives and knocks at the door of the sleeping ones? They awaken and are soon on their way.

Sura 50 Verse 9

9. And we send down from the sky rain charged with blessing, and we produce therewith gardens and grains for harvest.

You were indeed a land that was dead because the higher truth was missing from your life. This truth gives life to the land so that it flourishes. Through the expression of your godly qualities, you see the light within and it manifests above the land. It is like the sun in the sky. The light you can see within is God's light and from it, energy flows. The light is charged with blessings and wisdom to strengthen you. The land within has a garden into which the rains of Heaven fall. Within the garden are planted seeds of wisdom waiting to grow. As the raindrops moisturise the land they soften the seed's shell causing the casing to split. Once the casing has split, it releases what is inside where it can grow in the land. Be still and you will hear the whisperings from the droplets of wisdom. These words of wisdom will inspire you and your vision will become filled with all that you need to help you ascend to the station above you.

The pink light of love fertilises every part of your garden. The poetry from the seeds in your garden, fill you with a green light of growth. As the light from the wisdom gathers into a central sun within the land, it radiates all around you. You become as a lamp. As your garden radiates and fills with love, the angels bring more seeds, each containing beauty, each more beautiful than the last. Those of you who listen to the wisdom become as tall as the palm tree. You have your roots in the Earth, however, you tower high above the land.

As you resurrect yourself, you enter new states of awareness. Listen to your wisdom and use your ability to reason things out for yourself. Do not pass that responsibility to the intellect. Your reasoning is deeper than the intellect. Ponder on your inner wisdom. As you do, feel the inspiration, let it speak to you. Through your reasoning flows a river of wisdom. Behind your ability to reason is a power that flows from Heaven. When the love within you rises to the surface, the feelings of love that follow its arrival flow from Heaven. The things of the world you cling on to will vanish. If you hold onto negative energy, every so often it rises to the surface, exploding in little bursts. Behind reason, you will find reasonable thoughts. Before you engage in any experience, ask yourself, what is behind that door?

Read *Sura 6 Verse 122* and remember to raise yourself up and live within God's light and love. When you see the light, you will truly know you are on the right path. You can walk within the light. You can do this while living in a physical body. During your moments of *muraqabah*, you can visualise God's light flowing through your body. It heals, cleanses and re-balances your perception of the world. Indeed, from the light will come inspiration, signs and symbols to help you.

Truth comes to the door of the mind and knocks. Minds full of weeds produce more weeds, yet instead of weeds there could be roses. When you accept the seeds of wisdom planted in the garden, in your cultivation of them, changes take place and development flourishes. Take hold of the grains of truth, harvest and cultivate them. Nurture them, allowing them to grow. When you see the light on the screen of your mind, you will know it is indeed the gateway to Heaven. Through it, you will enter the garden and find peace, tranquillity and great beauty.

Read *Sura 7 Verse 40* and consider how can a camel pass through the eye of a needle? Certain thoughts and desires can expand you to the size of a camel. You know the way to the greater Heavens is through the light. You cannot get there by entertaining whatever thoughts you like. Only certain feelings and thought expressions are allowed to pass through the eye of the needle and into the light. Imagine for a moment you are walking along a tightrope carrying several poles to keep you balanced. The tightrope leads through a tunnel to a place of great beauty. However, due to the length of the poles you are carrying, you are unable to enter the tunnel. The tribe has convinced you that you will need the things they have given you to make the journey safely and you cannot get there without them. However, the people of the tribe who tell you to take these things with you have themselves never been there. Enjoy your life and by way of gratitude give thanks to God. Do this by sending out, from yourself, love and light. It is not a lot to ask in return for your gift of life. You must gain mastery, being able to make yourself great or small. It is here that you need strength of mind to keep your consciousness steady and stop it from swerving. You must learn to use your godly qualities wisely and as you fill yourself with love, you will find that you can travel with ease through the tunnel that leads to the Heavens.

Chapter 8: The Power of Your Thoughts

Sura 6 Verse 118
118. So, eat of (meats) on which God's name hath been pronounced,
if ye have faith in His signs.

Who else but God could express to humanity in such a beautiful way that our appetites for material gains can lead us astray? This is one of the many creative expressions used to expand your ability to reason things out for yourself.

Sura 6 Verse 119
119. Why should ye not eat of (meats) on which God's name hath been pronounced when He hath explained to you in detail what is forbidden to you.

You might think the verses above are in contradiction with each other; however, you should not look at these two verses with the same visual perception. They have been set like this to make you think beyond the words. This is where you can see that the wisdom from the evolved self can help you to separate and see what the irregularities do not.

The best meat you can eat is wisdom. The new food for thought that God feeds you, resurrects you. All that comes from the Heavens inspires you towards all that is good. You know the words of expression, which leave you bewildered. You should not eat these meats. They take words of light and restructure them. These words become devoid of light as they are devoured to become twisted in their expression and used by the irregularities to sway you from the truth.

Considering *Verse 118*, you must realise that all life is sacred and is not there for your enjoyment and consumption. All physical life has a spiritual opposite. As you expand your vision, you can see that the word *'meats'* does not apply only to the meat you eat. In *Verse 119*, it is telling you; *'not to eat of meats'*. People with the gift of prophecy can see what is about to manifest before it becomes clothed in physical matter. What God allows to manifest for one person is not right for everyone. Do not chase vigorously after what God has pronounced for another person or you will fall into ruin. If God is about to bestow wealth on someone, it is not for you to eat up a portion of that wealth. The things that are yours will arrive in your life according to the will of God.

Think about how people talk to you about their wants and desires. Many people deceive themselves by their appetites and false desires. When you listen to other people, compare what you hear with your own experiences of truth. Do not compare your life with what someone else is borrowing on their journey. Control your appetite and you will be healthier. Learn to balance your life. You will gain a great victory if you ignore the tribal self. You could spend all your life wanting something sent forth by the tribe and never receive it. They do indeed put forth promises to sway your vision. Think about the difference between; 'I want'; 'I wish'; and 'I am'. Use your ambition as a tool to raise your conscious awareness. You can manifest anything you wish when you are doing it for the right reasons. Many people do not check their thoughts or feelings but run mentally through life like a bull in a china shop. Running about chasing here and there does not necessarily bring you any closer to the things you want. Do not be hasty. Acts of self-restraint and forgiveness rewrite the record of your deeds.

Sura 2 Verse 155
155. Be sure we shall test you with something of fear and hunger some loss in goods or lives or the fruits (of your toil).

On your journey, do you pass without swerving or do you stop and stare? The rewards for the good decisions you have made will come back to you. When tested during the changeover of things, do not fall into doubt, thinking your hard work was all for nothing. When you have sufficiently surrendered to the light, you will transform to become lighter and brighter. In quiet times, the changeover is out with the old you, in with the new.

Be careful when you become involved in negative talk. It can quickly become an exaggerated sequence of events. There is the sequence as it really happens, the sequence you compare it against and the sequence you invent yourself. The illusion attaches itself to the illusion and has no power over the spiritual self. God is perfect and knows the exact measure of what you need to restore the record of your deeds.

Do not waste time thinking about what other people say or do. You are not responsible for their acts. Your questioning in the hereafter will be about your behaviour and the behaviour you encouraged in other people. It is not for you to fear your thoughts. Shift your focus to a happy place and dwell among the thoughts that create a place of beauty. Your thoughts have whatever strength you give them yourself. You can end up re-living events repeatedly because you keep giving them a life, a meaning, a purpose. God will send to you a light that will guide you.

Again, you can look at *Sura 21 Verse 102*. This is why it is so important to express loving thoughts. Love and a peaceful heart will smooth your journey home. You experience fears in the mind because of the direction you lean. God's love everywhere and in love, there is no fear. Look past the people who limit themselves to action and reaction. Your fears are a misdirected use of your emotions and feelings. Misdirection causes your vision to swerve, leading you astray. Work with love to bring light into the experiences. Once you have transformed the experience, you will be able to move forward on your journey. When you meditate, the lights you see are the lights of the Heavens. From the light flows inspiration that will impress on you what you need to know. It will cleanse you spiritually. The light draws you up in stages and contractions. You can become an expression of light and when you are in the light, you feel the love from the light. During your Earthly life, many thoughts that manifest from within the tribal self are the result of a conditioned association with something that is external to yourself. Governing laws preside over your life as it runs its course. You will know this by the variety of different ways the laws impress on you the intensity of the matter. Its impression is according to the record of your deeds. Added to this is the balance between your light and darkness. Use the following affirmation to help you grow in love with yourself, as well as other people.

I make a start.
My open heart
With every breath I take
Inside of me, God's energy
Dissolves, restores, I change.

When you use your thoughts to uplift yourself and other people, you will achieve greatness. If you make falsehoods fit into truth, eventually war breaks out within, pushing your brain faculty into overload. Time will help restore the imbalance that has occurred. Do not spend this time looking outwards, blaming other people. When the vision returns to you, what a shock you will get from what you see. There are no ifs or buts, only the truth. Some lessons are to slow you down in the pursuits that turn you away from your true centre. If you do not listen to your wisdom, what will it take to make you turn around? The simplest solution is the truth. The truth clears your conscience and restores a balance within you.

Sura 6 Verse 164
164. Every soul draws the meed of its acts on none but itself: no bearer of burdens can bear the burdens of another.

It is for you to cherish and love all who come into your vision. Even when you look at yourself, it is for you to express love and know that you must cherish yourself. You are divine. God created you and God is perfect. Accepting this truth and trusting in God is the surest way of transforming yourself. Embrace your trials and tests with love. In your world, the love that exists is according to your own loving desires. If you choose not to express love, God is not responsible for your swerving in error. In love, you are beautiful because you are perfection.

It is important to remember that all actions cause a reaction somewhere along the way. There is no escaping the Spiritual Law of Cause and Effect. If your fear of the truth is that other people do not accept you, surrender yourself. You must escape the tribal self's insanity instead of letting it impose itself on you. The tribal self is an accumulation of irregularities, which must be educated. The struggles and doubts you feel are a part of the reshaping process. It is the rising to the surface of a past acceptance, forgotten in this lifetime. For some people, it can be difficult and sad. They turn their backs on the inspiration sent to free them to satisfy the demands of the tribe.

For people who have been through a difficult period in their lives, with God all things are in ordered sequence. Use love, trust and truth. They are your foundation stones. Some people will see it straight away while others will have to search more deeply and for a longer period. With the acceptance of the first stepping-stone, peace will follow. Tread carefully and lay each foundation firmly, dismissing falsehoods as they present themselves.

Look a little more carefully before making a choice. In changing your mind, you have explored your options and are giving yourself an opportunity to choose greater wisdom. Your circumstances do not create your perception. Your thoughts create your perception. Allow yourself the time to be able to think things through before deciding. You owe it to yourself because no one else will care for you in the way you care for yourself.

Thoughts are not fleeting ideas in the mind. They are a living, breathing, pulsating energy. They contain sound and light. Energy follows thought and you become filled. If you do not try to learn, the moment of your passing will eventually arrive at your door, taking you home to the hereafter. You can make a great difference to your life right now. That difference starts with the desire to change, the desire to love all a little more. Take the chance because what waits for you on the other side of the changes will astound you.

Sura 55 Verse 9
9. So establish weight with justice and fall not short in the balance.

When balancing 'weight with justice' in the verse above, what is sent forth from the tribe will weigh you down with burdens. Through the evolved self, inspiration flows and as you sail with a favourable wind, you climb the degrees of conscious awareness. You must fulfil certain requirements before you can cross the firmament that He has raised high. Indeed, you will detect this as a kind of crossing point, or bridge. If you fall short in the requirements, you will not traverse this place of crossing. Transform the three veils of darkness and raise your consciousness. As you express loving feelings, you attract the attention of God. He adds to your feelings, sending inspiration to you as a way of showing you the truth about His promise to you. He shows you what purifies and raises you. As you oversee all matters in your world, what comes through the light will help you to decide on the best course of action to pursue.

How has God established His plan so that irregularity does not outstride the light? He has assigned to and established within each of us a due balance. One half of this balance we call the light. The other half we call the darkness. It is through your loving desires to know that you read books of inspiration. It is through an even greater love within you that you recognise what is here and apply yourself. An even greater love allows you to see beyond these words. You can look within, follow the truth and trust and apply your feelings. In front of you will manifest a beautiful light. As you continued to listen to the inner loving truths, they disperse the crowds of irregularity and doubt. The truth will come to you as a small insight within the conscious self. It is for you to understand and develop this insight into a full flame of bright beauty.

Nothing happens that does not give you an opportunity to aspire towards a self-transformation. In the different roles you enter, there are truths and lessons to learn. People who embark on a religious role should not look out at life believing all must succumb to the role they are playing. All life is on a spiritual journey of learning and self-discovery. Stepping into a particular role or character may present a feeling of loving desires for you. However, other roles people play, present fulfilment in accordance with the experiences they need as they travel their journey, learn their lessons and open their awareness. Whatever you do, Spiritual Laws govern and balance its expression in your life. You eventually reach the end of the lesson. You then connect to another stream and flow along according to how God's Spiritual Laws govern the lesson and its expression in your life.

You are a co-creator and as you enter the manifestations, you learn through direct experience. Do not let your irregularities influence you into thinking that you have no choice or freewill. The Law of Freewill always grants you freedom of choice. Find a balance for your emotional logic and do not let it become a negative emotion. Feelings and self-restraint transform what arises from base matter. You are only limited in options because of the thoughts you choose to believe in. As a part of our interaction with the physical world, there are certain conditionings that we have accepted into our lives. The first time you hear something, it does not make it absolute truth. Do not be the thirsty fool. The ordered sequence of events in your life has been set up to help you. Thoughts build a foundation on which you can stand. Be prepared to change the old with the new.

A closer examination of yourself will show you that your character is made up of habits, manners, mannerisms and gestures, all of which you accepted. The only rules about them are the rules you make yourself. If something can be changed or introduced into your life, such as a mannerism it cannot be the real you. Your mannerism is something you have chosen to identify yourself with while you live your Earthly life. It is something you see other people doing and so you imitate them. Your character, even the language you speak is but an extension of the society you have chosen to enter. If you think of yourself as a house and you turn yourself upside down. All that falls out is all that you have put in. These are your fittings. All the fixtures are your personality traits. Fixtures are the things that stay in the house when you turn it upside down. The following is a list of some of the fixtures within your house. Love, truth, trust, forgiveness, self-restraint, kindness, compassion, determination, courage, strength and surrender, to name but a few. Think of the ninety-nine names of God. These are all things associated to your spiritual self. They form the fixtures within you that exist in varying degrees of development.

Your spirit and soul are not the same. The soul is a fixture within the spirit. Spirit is your divine self, the part of you that is pure energy. Your soul contains your personality; it is like a flame within the spirit. The things you learn and accept are your fittings. Your soul's personality can change. On one occasion you may be outgoing and extrovert, on another occasion, you may be a shy person and introvert. Between these two personalities there are many unique variations giving each of us our own personality. Indeed, your spirit is like the arc that carries the soul. You cross the bridge between the physical world and the spiritual world. There is also a crossing from the spiritual world to the physical. Think of it like your brain, which controls your body, yet it is only a small part of the whole. For you to grow and develop, you have to flow with favourable winds. It is within the flow that you extract good things to eat. As you choose what you will accept as true, it becomes a part of you. Your inner light will redefine your purpose in life. When you stop loving, you stop growing. Beyond what you ascribe to yourself, there is a spiritual world to explore. It is a spiritual world of complete awareness.

Within the Heavens, there is access to many worlds and there are many conscious spiritual beings. If you listen with a tentative ear, they may speak to you. Let their grains of wisdom grow in the garden. It is your job to choose what you cultivate. In your surrender and acceptance of trust and truth, you restore a balance. God's love reaches each person. His light guides you and what is contained within the light teaches you. A kind word from the light of your inner self can reach places within you and others that a gift from the material world cannot.

We come into this world to experience its substance in a way that surrounds us on all sides. Your immersion in the world of physical matter is according to your book of deeds. For many people, a greater part of what brings about an awareness of the hereafter is undeveloped until the person is ready, yet you are always ready.

It is for each of us to transform into light the base matter into which we are born. You are here to experience life according to the needs of your inner self and not according to your so-called needs for material gain. Do not rush into things without looking, in the pretence that you have a visual or hearing defect, especially when you think there is a gain for you. Your own eager thoughts tell you to rush in, whereas your awareness may tell you to withhold yourself and wait. Use the following affirmation to connect with your light.

> To bring about a balance
> I must bring about a change.
> To the thought within my mind
> I'll use the light to re-arrange.

Your loving feelings are the winds that blow against the sails of your ship. As the wind blows against them, what is contained within you drives you along the pathway you call your destiny. As you travel, let irregularity teach you to hold yourself steady in the light. Sadness teaches you to be happy. Feeling unloved teaches you that you need to spread love. Practise *muraqabah*, listening to your own trust and truth. You already know the words and feelings of expression that will take you on your journey into the light.

Chapter 9: Balance, Heal and Protect

As you get to know yourself in relation to the verses of *The Quran*, you can restore a balance to yourself.

Sura 38 Verse 36
36. Then we subjected the wind to his power, to flow gently to his order, whithersoever he willed.

Meditation enhances one's awareness and being aware is the key to working with the subtle energies that interconnect our world from the other dimensions. You experience this energy as a wave or it reaches you as a stream that maintains its flow. The loving vibrations within the energies hold a balancing and healing.

Healing is the transmission of energy. It is the balancing of energy where imbalance has occurred. It is restoration and the bringing about of harmony to things that have fallen into discord. It is the process whereby a person or object is used as a conduit or vessel through which energies are transmitted. Energy flows in one end, flows out the other and transforms as it travels. Healing energies restore the balance of both men and women, objects and places where there has been a build-up of irregular vibrational confusion.

The verse above is from a story about Solomon. The wind that is subject to his order is the subtle spiritual energy of God. In other words, the energy of God would flow in whichever direction Solomon turned his attention.

The healing energy that is subject to Solomon is not a harsh energy like the kind sent forth by people who dwell within their irregularities. The energy sent forth is a wind that is gentle, kind and loving. His internal vision shows him what is taking place as he works spiritually, with love to bring back into harmony and balance, what has fallen out of alignment and into discord.

When you set your intention and direct your focus of attention to the sending from yourself of loving feelings, the angelic forces are aware of your spirit's expression. They will draw close to you. In this, you will know that the garden of Heaven is close to you. As you direct and send out love to the stated destination of your choice, as the energy flows through you, you receive healing as well.

Read *Sura 3 Verse 112* and consider how shame can be pitched over someone like a tent of darkness. What disperses the darkness is the manifestation of love. Love is a divine expression of a godly quality. Many gifts within the expression of love will reveal themselves to you. When all you have is love, you want to share it with other people. We each have the ability to send to another person, this loving energy that balances, heals, soothes, restores and protects. When in your inner house, you visualise the light of God surrounding, balancing and healing someone, his or her greater self accepts this loving kindness from you.

Read *Sura 83 Verse 14* and when you sit in *muraqabah*, send light to those who are ill; those who are finding life difficult. Doing so, you are able to assist in their protection and wellbeing. The loving energies you send forth can help in the restoration, healing and balance of the person you hold in your mind's eye.

In everyday life and learning, no one really teaches you about healing your inner self or the violence of thoughts and its effect on others and on you. If you could see the harm that you do to yourselves and other people, when you think negative thoughts, you would refrain. Remember what you wish on other people is first wished on your own self. When you visualise light surrounding yourself or other people, this light creates a protective shield that deflects the lower vibrational energies sent forth by those who dwell within their irregularities.

Sura 51 Verses 1-3
1. By the (winds) that scatter broadcast;

2. And those that lift and bear away heavy weights;
3. And those that flow with ease and gentleness;

Boasting and gossip is nothing more than a scorching wind that scatters the hearts of all those involved. It causes mischief in the land and what is green and fertile becomes a barren desert.

When you first retreat into your own inner sacred mosque, you will find yourself surrounded by the darkness. As you continue, the scattered broadcast that caused you mischief soon becomes a soothing wind. Within the darkness, there will come the beautiful lights of Heaven.

Everybody knows the destination; they want to go to *Janna* (Heaven). You know your thoughts and actions play an important part in getting you to where you want to be. You can ask yourself now and again; 'Is what manifests within befitting of someone who will be invited to be a resident of the Heavens?' By finding a balance between what is physical and what is spiritual, a healing will take place within. To aid the process you need a strategy that works, and meditation works. Within the stillness, you detect the movement of the subtle vibrational energies. You can use this energy, directing it around yourself, to cleanse and balance your whole self. You can share this energy with other people. As you share this love and light, you start to work for the benefit and profit of humanity. Truly, spirit and spiritual work is the patterning and the handiwork of God.

One thing that stays with you all the time is the truth. You may adopt many labels and apply them to yourself as to whom you think you are. However, you are so much more. Do not only plan your material journey; also implement thoughts into your life that will work for you on your spiritual journey.

The healing of yourself is a delicate matter. It is best if you are in a state of surrender and calmness, as this will put you in a more receptive mood to receiving the healing energy of love. When you are out of balance, you become dis-eased. You fall out of alignment with the streams of energy that fully revitalises your spiritual and physical self.

There exists a destructive energy and an energy that rebuilds. The destructive energy is not necessary out of alignment with the truth. This energy breaks things down so that the new flourishes. A part of your learning is to understand how to self-manage the irregularities that show up within your mind. If there were not a breaking down process, how could there exist a rebuilding process. For something to transform, it must first be broken down.

You can see this going on in your life right now. Some of your experiences may have broken you down mentally, but from there, as a result, you have rebuilt yourself, reinvented yourself. From these experiences, you gain wisdom because you now look a little longer before you leap.

Remember the body is a conduit through which energy can flow. If you hold on to irregular thoughts and do not release them using the proper faculties and channels, the energy will seek its own means of escape. Like water, the energy will look for the weakest point that will allow it to run its course. Some of the symptoms, when there is a leaning in the mind in the direction of the more destructive energies, are confusion and doubt, anxiety and depression, illness and exhaustion.

Some of the illnesses in the body are there to let you know on a physical level that there is a spiritual matter, which needs addressing. You need to learn how to heal yourself through the construction of light energy. Is it that your old foundation built on the sand cliffs has been washed away? Your feelings of despair come from the crumbling down of what you have built. Choose with love and God will establish another foundation that is stronger than the previous one. Then will He open a door that allows you to continue your journey. The old must be swept away before the new can establish itself. If you do not choose right, negative energy keeps building up within you until it explodes in little bursts and expressions.

The mind allows you to see what is within yourself. It plays inspiration like a movie on the screen of your mind. You see this through your mind's eye. As you did in the meditation exercises, examine your physical body using your inner vision. If you intuitively see a dark spot, you can manifest a light to disperse the unwanted energy. It could be that the energy you see is about to express itself through your physical body as an illness, pain or stiffness or another condition. Learn to become aware of your body and look after it with light and love. Look at all the issues within yourself and deal with the pain sensitively, lovingly, and a little bit at a time.

Healing energy comes in many different colours, each colour a vibration that holds within its centre an essence to embrace and rebalance you. The green tree of life spoken about in many Holy books and mentioned in *The Quran* shows there are similarities between different religions. Your task, as part of your development and growth, is to kindle the flame, the fire of your own spirit. It is also worth noticing from which direction you kindle that fire. One direction gives you the appearance of royalty the other darkens you. Read *Sura 36 Verse 80* for further enlightenment.

We each receive energy, however, because this energy is of a finer or lighter vibration, to detect its presence you must lighten and brighten yourself. Connect with what is gathered and harvested for you. For those of you who detect this spiritual harvest, they will be aware of a downloading into their conscious awareness of spiritual wisdom. As you follow its course and expand on its truth, you gain spiritual insight. Alternatively, are you looking in the wrong direction and not seeing anything? Or, are you like a whirlwind bringing destruction to the houses around you?

The deeper you enter into your inner-sacred mosque the greater will be the wisdom you retrieve. It is for you to open what comes to you and read. For many of you, there will be an angel waiting there with a message and a blessing for you.

As you begin to work with this information, you begin to grow and expand into a full flame of bright beauty. It is through God's grace and your own thinking, feeling and willpower that you grow. Turn what you hear from the darkness into something you can use in the process of elevating yourself. You are the cherisher and it is by your own will that you can produce from the light or the darkness, fruit or weeds as you make a choice. You then sail your own ship on the sea, in surrender, to your stated destination.

When you decide to go within and meditate, at times the light is so bright that you turn away as if almost blinded by its beauty. As you cycle back into the irregular activity, you stand still, afraid, as you sink into the depths of self-pity and victim mode. However, do not fall into despair; the angels and in the hereafter see your striving. The loving energies that flow through them to you, fills you with many blessings, which realign the patterning of your whole being. The light that manifests disperses the irregular programmes and this has an effect on the physical matter coverings. Physical things can heal and rebalance as the energy realigns and reprograms its infrastructure. Through your own will, if you sustain the loving expression, you will arrive at a station through which new insights will manifest.

Sura 35 Verse 12
12. Nor are the two bodies of flowing water alike.

From which body of water do you express yourself and your words? One is filled with love and the other filled with irregularities. As you drink, you fill with either ornaments of a swirling mist or the bright ornaments of light and love. Your task here is to know from which rivers you drink your fill because each may produce before you an alluring gift.

In the same way there is food for the body, there is food for your inner self. Your physical food becomes your physical body in the same way your thoughts become the garments for your spirit self. Read *Sura 74 Verse 4* in support of this passage.

Allow the melody from you to express itself in love. Let your inner vision seek out that part of you that needs healing. What plagues your mind has arisen to the surface so it may receive its healing. Realise your true spiritual potential and live your life as a spiritual being living in a physical world. Learn to work with the colours you see in your meditations. As you dwell within your loving expression, you will receive all you need to initiate a balancing and healing, leading to a transformation and change.

Sura 21 Verse 80
80. It was we who taught him the making of coats of mail for your benefit, to guard you from each other's violence: Will ye then be grateful?

God taught Solomon how he could protect himself against the violence other people sent against him. This violence was not always physical but spiritual. There is the violence of thought-related activity. When we think loving thoughts, we create and send out from ourselves loving energy. This energy first fills us and surrounds us. The love and guidance you receive from the inner core essence of the light will protect you from the violence of other people's thoughts.

God and the angels watch over both men and women who practise spellcasting, which creates mischief. Certain people you go to will have you believe they are the ones who make things right. However, is what you ask of them true to the light and love of your inner self, or are you swayed by insecurities, fear of loss and suspicious gossip? Read *Sura 2 Verse 155* and consider how your fears of disappointments rise to the surface, especially during your trials and tests. If you dwell on your irregular thoughts, they will turn against you. There are certain people who choose to create evil thoughts, they whisper into the hearts of other people. They bid them to do wrong and in a weak moment of hesitation, many have fallen. Many senders or creators of envy do not stay around once their manifest thoughts of error go out. They withdraw back into their shell.

Before we move on, let us look at another interpretation of a verse from *The Quran* that will help you disperse irregular activity. It comes from the same Yusuf Ali translated version. However, the meaning of the verse is expressed differently. This version is by the Department of Islamic Researchers printed at the King Fahd printing complex.

Sura 113 Verse 4

Translates as:
> *'From the mischief of those who blow on knots;'*

While another version translates as:
> *'From the mischief of those who practice secret arts'.*

Those who *'blow on knots'* and use their freewill to enforce an irregular matter, usually do so for material gains. However, greater is it to their loss. The person or group of people who ask for such a matter to be manifest reap shares in the creation. It will be gathered up and redistributed among those wrong doers involved. You can disperse an evil spell that is cast using light and love. Let us have a look at something you can do.

Disperse Irregularities Exercise

- Take some string or something similar about the same thickness as a shoelace.

- Tie a bow, not too tight, in the lace for each of your problems. Think about the month it started.
- Once you have tied the bows.
- Hold the string by the ends and say a small prayer.
- Slowly pull the ends of the string apart so the bows start to undo.
- Fill yourself with love before each bow completely unties.
- As they undo, blow on them three times, visualising the problems dissolving or transforming into a light and dispersing.
- Once all the bows have opened, bury the string in the Earth, sprinkling over the top a little sea salt.
- Leave it to rot in the ground.
- A good time to do this is on a full moon and at 12:00 o'clock midnight as one day passes into another.

Use this daily affirmation to confirm your actions and intentions.

May the silent breath of light and love
Dissolve the whispers of darkness.
As the moon crosses time, as the night becomes the day
May all thought forms of evil be washed away.

There is no great mystery about how to protect yourself. It takes a thought to beat a thought. This is why the expression of love in your life is so important. Another way of protecting yourself is simple and takes only a few minutes each day. See *Sura 6 Verse 65* and *Sura 21 Verse 80*.

Protect Yourself Exercise

- Close your eyes and visualise a light surrounding you like a bubble.
- See light filling the bubble and swirling through and around you, filling every part of your body.

- See the light wash away any negative energy, which you can send down into the Earth where it will be naturalised.
- Then encircle this bubble of light with a golden light.
- See the ends joining and lock into place around you.
- If a negative thought tries to penetrate your bubble of protection, the golden light will deflect it.
- The thought bounces off you and back to the sender.
- As you become aware of such thoughts, instead of sending back what you received, send back loving thoughts. This will strengthen you and will help the sender.

For you to work according to God's patterning, work in a loving way. To be a healer is to recognise you are spiritual energy and be aware of the flow of energy. God's loving universal energy is transferable from one person to another. Energy flows from spirit, through your spirit, to their spirit. As you reduce your burdens, you are able to take on more responsibility, aiding other people in the release of their burdens. You are able to help with the restoration, balancing, healing and protection of other people. Refer to *Sura 34 Verse 49*, which indicates that indeed, those who dwell within the darkness never restore anything. Those who dwell on high know that burdens are nothing more than false desires and imposed conditionings created by irregularity.

If you choose to be of service and work to lift away the ills of another, disperse what is heavy using love, wisdom and the light of God. As the light disperses the irregular energy, within the receiver grows a feeling of wellbeing.

Apologising to God and yourself for the slip when you create an irregularity is the surest way of defusing what you have sent forth. Express love and reap the rewards of what you send out. Love has many more advantages and is unlimited. Love is one of the universal forces that bonds and unites us all together as one.

The projection of your consciousness is not limited and can allow you to travel great distances. Here is a personal experience of this. Once while thinking about how big the universe is, in a matter of seconds my consciousness projected outwards. It arrived at the outer edges of our star system where the furthest stars were. Where my consciousness had come to rest, our galaxy was expanding at a tremendous speed. There was a great void before me. Gazing into this void there were no stars within it. It was empty yet it was alive. There was no end to this void. This place was the beginning of something more. Whole galaxies could have quite easily fit into this space, each one like a drop of water in an ocean.

The speed of thought is instantaneous. You are a manifester of thought, which makes you more than the thought. As thoughts can transport you anywhere, imagine if you were to go beyond the thought and really get to know yourself. As pure spirit, you can go beyond the zones of Heaven. Read *Sura 55 Verse 33* and consider how spirit is beyond the light of the Heavens, for the light is a manifestation of love. Love is an expression and manifestation of spirit.

When you send thoughts of love to another person, they receive them with great joy. They may not be as fortunate as you are. You can assist in the protection of other people. When you come across someone whose burden is heavy, if they have trouble seeing beyond that burden; have a little compassion. It is the task of each of us to find a way of helping others and making ourselves lighter and brighter. You have the ability to create within you, a garden full of radiance and beauty. As you dwell within your inner garden, its essence will express itself through you. Here are two small *zikrs*; one for other people and one for you. For example, if you wish God's love and light on another, your subconscious accepts that this is what you wish to create as a reality. Therefore, it accepts this as something to be produced in your life. The first affirmation is for other people, the second one for you.

Let light and love heal their soul.
Protecting them from thoughts of old.
Dispersing what darkens life.
When they are in the midst of strife.

Let light and love heal my soul.
Protecting me from thoughts of old.
Dispersing what darkens life.
When I am in the midst of strife.

Sura 10 Verse 27
27. But those who have earned evil will have a reward of like evil:

Where do the ideas you live your life by come from? Do they come through the evolved self? Are they from people who mix up their truth? Do they form out of who you think you are because of the society you were born into? Do those around you who feed you your life plans really have your best interests in their heart? Is the wrongdoing they do piled one on top of the other over their inner light? Did their plan come through the light or is it a product of their own creation to suppress you? Is the energy they share beautiful in its expression? It is within your own self where you should look for answers. You have to decide if what comes to you is limiting or expansive and creative, flowing, productive and graceful. Most importantly, does it include love, trust and truth? If you choose to follow the untruth rather than the truth, you follow something other than God's original divine plan He creates for you.

One way of keeping you restrained is to give you a life plan that goes nowhere. You do not have to keep the same plan for the rest of your life. There is no harm in making a few modifications. If you are not making progress, it is usually because of some thoughts you are afraid to let go.

Change the direction you face and pay attention, listening to that silent voice within. It will help you to change the course of your life.

You can learn to live and express yourself from within its deeper pools of light. In time, the loving truth and trust will disperse the dark crowd and you will enter the inner garden. Do not be a person who says; 'What is this?' but be someone who says; 'Huh! What is that?' Truly, you will marvel at what you see. As you command a sight of all things, you will see visions of your true destiny. You will come to know God's divine plan is working itself out through your life.

You will be rewarded for your striving, practising patience, firmness and self-restraint. As you look within, signs and symbols give you guidance out of the darkness. They may also be a warning because they show you things to come that are most terrible. Truly, God's words and His work will succeed according to the spiritual teaching of *The Quran*, as written in *Sura 41 Verse 53*. Some people who refuse to listen to the calling from within will be in a sad state when called to account. For sure, a reprieve gives each of us another chance to make amends and complete our journey. However, why wait when you can start the process of transformation today.

Through contemplation and surrendering, you transcend the states of consciousness you are at present residing within. Incorporating love and meditation into your life plan will raise you up in nearness to all that is good. If you have a business and it is not doing well, you do not waste time making changes to help it on its way. Follow the inner inspiration and make the necessary changes to advance your growth. You can change how you interpret and understand the things taught to you. *The Quran* has a message to help you expand and grow. Where there is a growth in love, there is a growth in understanding. If you do not listen and reflect, extracting from the light, the fullness of all that is there, how will you fully know, understand and learn so that you can complete your journey. Do not let inspiration stay behind a wall of thought activity. A part of the guidance from the wisdom of your inner self will be about looking after you, protecting you from the whispers of irregularity.

As you surrender your will, you move towards and enter the Holy land.

God is the planter of what you must kindle. The fires you kindle are your own godly qualities that build up your inner light to give you a firm foundation on which to stand.

One of the reasons why this world has been set up is to allow beings of varying degrees of light and darkness to come together in one place. As you make comparisons between one thought and another, you must choose. If you choose the light, follow its course. To reach the station above, you have to make a determined effort to leave the comfort zone where you dwell.

Chapter 10: Adam and Eve

Consider *Sura 2 Verses 35-36* and the story about Adam and Eve. It is also worth remembering that the word garden also applies to the garden of the inner self.

Firstly, the reason why God created was because there was no one to know Him except Himself; so out of Himself He created.

If there is no one to know you then you will not fully know yourself. It is through your interactions with external things to yourself that you are able to measure the depth, breadth and width of yourself. As you meditate and explore your own inner apartments, you get to know with greater clarity the depth, breadth and width of your inner self.

As you think about the story of Adam and Eve, you will realise that the story is expressing something about the creation of the human race, of the masculine and feminine spiritual energy. Adam is the name given to the masculine energy and Eve the name given to the feminine energy. You will also find that as you explore your own inner self, the masculine has something of the feminine and the feminine has something of the masculine energy.

The easiest way to explain our original spiritual creation was to express it through the form of a story. Into such stories of old is weaved a meaning deeper and wider than many people can perceive. Over a long period, we lost sight of the spiritual wisdom that keeps open our awareness about the events in the hereafter. We only saw the words in relation to the physical world forms as we explored the lands we inhabited. The story of Adam and Eve is not a story to read with a vision directed towards the physical reality. Many people understand the stories through the limitations of awareness as we became clothed in matter. Their story was a way of grounding and anchoring a spiritual event into the minds of those on Earth. The stories that you read in *The Quran* have an inner wisdom only seen when inspiration opens your eyes. The question you need to ask yourself is; 'Are these stories based on physical world events? Or are they spiritual events clothed in stories that we might remember through inspiration?' *The Quran* keeps saying to you at the end of some parables; '... *that you might remember or those who can read'*. Some people grasp the inner meaning and as stories, we can all understand them in varying degrees.

Some stories are like your dreams. Many of the things you see yourself doing in your dreams are activities that relate to the material world. However, hidden from the view of many people is the spiritual message that you can extract for a deeper understanding. With the expansion of your conscious awareness and the power of your ability to reason things out for yourself, your inner vision is able to see into the stories of *The Quran*.

Sura 4 Verse 1
1. O mankind! Reverence your Guardian-Lord, who created you from a single person.

Also refer to *Sura 39 Verse 6*. God has no need of a partner as God is self-sustaining and because there is only one God, His first creation was the light and the darkness. Following that, He created the Holy Spirit. *Sura 2 Verse 87, Sura 2 Verse 253, Sura 5 Verse 113* and *Sura 16 Verse 102*. From spirit, came a single person, from which came forth the masculine energy and the feminine energy. The masculine energy that was to become one-half of the human-race was given the name Adam and the feminine energy was given the name Eve. The inner core essence of Adam is truth. The inner core essence of Eve is trust. When God looked on His creation and His creation looked back, a loving energy began to spread out. This loving energy would become one of the essences that forever unites each of us to the other.

The love between God and His creation grew, ever deepening, ever expanding. Adam and Eve lived in this love, bathed in this love. As they went out into God's creation, they began to explore. The masculine and feminine energies were joined. However, they eventually grew apart and became independent of each other.

Traditional Christians know the Holy Spirit as the Holy Ghost. The Holy Spirit is the spirit of inspiration through which we receive what God wants to reveal. God has no partners because He is self-sustaining, so there can be no Trinity. Each of the elements that man has associated to the Trinity is separate. God is God. Spirit is spirit. God created what we call spirit and it is from this spirit energy, He created male and female.

Here are a number of Suras for you to look at that support this, starting with *Sura 6 Verse 1*, *Sura 16 Verse 102*, and the previously mentioned *Sura 4 Verse 1*. *Sura 16 Verse 8* and *Sura 36 Verse 36*, which explains God created things of which we have no knowledge. You also have to take into account the zones beyond what we call Heaven. This includes the angelic realms. On Earth, you have the animal kingdoms, large and small. Humankind is but one of many spiritual forms God has created. *Sura 6 Verse 38* mentions, each different kind of animal is part of a community like humanity. *Sura 76 Verse 1* makes it clear that there was a time when humankind did not even exist.

Let us look at some kind of order of creation. First is God. Second the light and the darkness. Third is the Holy Spirit/Ghost, the spirit of inspiration through which God's revelations come. Forth is the form we know as spirit, the single person which can be seen in Sura 4 Verse 1, Sura 6 Verse 109, Sura 7 Verse 198 and Sura 39 Verse 6 for those who have the vision. Fifth is Adam and Eve created from the single person. Sixth is our spirit form, created from Adam and Eve. Thus, if you want to associate sons and daughters, then our true parents are Adam and Eve, the masculine and feminine energy. You also have to take into account God created the seven Heavens and the Earth. *The Quran* also speaks of worlds and not world. God is far beyond the form of spirit of which He created each of us. How can that which has been created be equal with its creator?

Before our creation, God created the light and the darkness. However, there are places beyond what we call Heaven and its light. Read *Sura 55 Verse 33* as it explains to us the ultimate challenge and that is to pass beyond the zones of Heaven and Earth. There are realms of spirit we have yet to explore. What we think of as Heaven and its light is but a zone within God's kingdom. The place we call Heaven and the light was created through the expression of love.

We are not the physical body, neither are we the light. Both are manifestations of spirit. To us, God is the light. However, He is not the light itself. He is beyond the light, beyond our spiritual self. The light is God's way of showing Himself to us. God created the light so that we have a direction in which to strive. It would be hard for us to mentally identify, relate or perceive God if He did not present Himself to us in some form. He chose light as the vehicle through which He would show Himself to us. In this way or through the light, we are able to feel a connection with Him. When we see the light, we know which direction we need to focus our attention. Through the light, we receive inspiration and knowledge about the processes that helps us to make the journey back to spirit. Remember, between man and God there are seventy thousand veils of light. Each of us has a light within. This light gives each one of us our uniqueness and keeps open our connection to the heavens. As we feel the love flow through the light, it completely fills us. It is through our development and expression of love that we ascend up to the Heavens. We can reach out to God through the light as it runs before us. We will discuss God's light again in Chapter 12, Seeking God's Face.

Be kind to your Earthly parents but hold in understanding your true spiritual farther and mother, for the real womb from which you came forth is Adam and Eve, the masculine and feminine energy.

Your parents in this world are but a means through which you enter into this physical reality. It is then up to you, how you make your journey. We are all spiritual brothers and sisters, spiritual beings, and have a spiritual form that many people know not, unless they turn their attention inwardly and reflect in the mind.

You will find that God is a God of perfect equality. He created all things in equal proportion and nothing is any lesser than another is. Certain beliefs have caused many to fall into the programmed conditioning that one is not equal to another. Your children are no lesser than you are because they are born out of you, in the same way, you are born out of your mother and father and you are no lesser than they are. Do your wants in the material world cause you to lose sight of God's Spiritual Law of Equality, which you should be striving to implement? There is no more blame on one than on another. In Islam, there is no original sin and each one of us is accountable for our own deeds and actions.

We are alive in spirit before we entered into this world of matter and we will return to the hereafter. Meditation gives you a chance to realise your true spiritual self as a reality. Remember, *The Quran* is a book for all men and women, explaining the spiritual journey they must all one day make. All the teaching that the prophets brought into the world will help you to expand your awareness. The Holy books explain we are all on a journey and we must each deal with our own burdens as we sail through the great spiritual oceans.

There is clarification in *The Quran* that tells us before we came to this Earth we were living as spiritual beings. This leads us on to conclude that we came to this physical world from the spiritual world. Some people believe that our spirit only came into existence after our birth in the physical world. In the hereafter, we are aware of our life's plan and our Earthly experiences before we come here. Our spirit comes forth from Heaven to experience a life in the physical world. Spiritual experiences are a natural reality; it is the spiritual being in human form that is becoming aware of its own inner essence. Think carefully about this next verse.

Sura 2 Verse 36
36. We said: "Get ye down, all (ye people), with enmity between yourselves."

The Adam and Eve story is not a myth but a simple way of explaining the creation and beginning of the human race. If they, the people, are being sent forth to the world because of an event that took place, then they must have been residing somewhere else before being sent. Not only does this verse tell us we were somewhere else, it tells us more than two of us slipped from the grace of God. Nothing has changed, as God's ways do not change. We are still coming from the Heavens and the spiritual world into the physical world to amend the record of our deeds. Seeking the kingdom of Heaven brings you into contact with those who reside in Heaven. *The Quran* talks about seeking the home of the hereafter in *Sura 33 Verse 29.*

Read *Sura 24 Verses 35-36,* and you will see that the key to understanding these verses is in the second verse, where it says; *'lit is such a light in houses'.* For you must remember that your body is the house of your spirit. Within each spirit is a light. Through this light, each spirit receives substance. Some lights are lighter and brighter than others are. This spiritual force within you emits a light. This light brightens up the darkness around you. The light force is your direct connection to the hereafter.

Our bodies are a niche through which the spirit expresses itself. As the light within us shines, it is like a light from a lantern. Our bodies are as fragile as the glass that surrounds the lantern. In dark places, the glass helps to reflect and distribute the lantern's inner light. The glass now takes on another role where the niche is now the veil between the spiritual and the physical world. It is there, yet it is not there. Some people can hear and see through this veil, other people pick and choose, the rest ignore what is sent as inspiration. Our inner essence is like a brilliant star, but our enclosure into limited time and space causes our perception of the light to grow dim.

There is a divine light residing within each one of us and we have all the faculties we need to change the small light into a full flame of bright beauty. *Sura 17 Verses 20-21* talks about when you have many lamps together, some contain more fuel than others do; yet each started out as a small light. You are the one who must light the flame within. As you fill with light on light, so too are the parables of *The Holy Quran*. As you build your light on light, Heaven reveals its hidden delights as your vision gains a greater universal sweep.

When you think about a niche and how something can exist within something else as a comfortable environment, when this is applied to ourselves. Each one of us lives and breathes as a niche in both the physical and the spiritual worlds. As you move through the degrees, passing into the greater states, each degree is a niche within a niche.

As a way of further helping you to understand this gathering of thoughts, remember the three main states of consciousness, including the: conscious self; subconscious self; and unconscious self. As you begin to customise yourself to the ways of the world and the society you have become a part of, other states of consciousness come into existence. One is the tribal zone or the tribal self and the other is the evolved self, or higher self.

Each state has many degrees within its polarity. In *The Quran*, each degree is a river. As you travel through these degrees and around these states, the Spiritual Laws govern you. Each one of us resides within a particular degree or state of consciousness within the boundaries and polarity assigned to us.

You will have an idea about where you are residing within your polarity, according to the way you feel and the impressions you see as thoughts and images imprint themselves on the screen of your mind. As you oversee the inner activity, your truth, trust, reason, wisdom and understanding will be there to preside over each manifested thought and vision.

When you project yourself in the wrong direction, the reflection that comes back to you is from the tribal self. The more you feed this shadow, the stronger it will become within you. It is you yourself that gives birth to this tribal zone or this tribal self, which opens the door through which more irregularities can flow. When you step into this shadow, it reduces your vision of things in the greater states of awareness. You enter this tribal zone, which sets itself up to become an opposing force against God's love and will. It expresses itself as judge and jury over all things that do not fit into its limited vision. When you create from within the inner sanctuary of the tribal zone, if you accept what manifests, as you feed it, it grows to become an active force within you. Surely, you lead yourself astray if you do not learn how to manage its expression. The question is how much of your energy do you feed to it? Do you choose to accept its suggestions and override the wisdom of the wise one who calls you to all that is good?

When you enter the light of the subconscious self, the things that are so important to the tribal self are greatly subdued in strength. As you reside within the unconscious, if you hear what comes from the tribe at all, it is but the remains of an echo heard from a place so close, yet so far.

It is through your own efforts that you send forth your consciousness. As you sail on the ocean, you are blown by a favourable wind. As you come to rest and hold yourself steady in the stillness, the veil that covers your view slowly rises. This happens in stages and contractions. In meditation, the light and the land you see before you will eventually become your home for a while. When you set sail again, you enter a different ocean and sail your ship. The wind is different on this ocean. What you know will wilt and die. The new knowledge you extract, expands and builds within you a new understanding by which you guide yourself.

As you walk on sacred ground and stand in the presence of God, seeds of wisdom enter you from the light. In your acceptance of these gifts, as you fertilise the seeds with your presence, they flourish within your garden, quickly reaching a state of harvest. What is good for you, grounds you in truth, expanding you in love and wisdom. From there you are able to explore what is beyond irregular thought. You grow to become the best version of yourself.

True love brings true awareness taking away all doubts. Love frees you from the constraints of the tribal self. The light easily finds its way into the tribal self. As you raise yourself from this station, it is as if you have emigrated because you now live in a land far beyond irregularity. When you take your leave of the physical world, you will enter the hereafter, returning to the place you created through good deeds.

There are certain thoughts that expand or reduce your vision. If you do not work to expand your awareness, developing your inner vision, you will be like the blind person in the presence of people who can see.

As you develop your inner vision, you see the angels who watch over you. They teach you how best to walk your pathway. You will find that you are able to live your life with the awareness that the guidance you are given is true. The hereafter was there all the time. It was through the beliefs you held that limitations blinded you to its existence. You will receive wisdom, which brings new knowledge to the garden, and instead of being dead to spiritual expression and experiences, you become alive and filled with wonder.

Sura 2 Verse 38
38. We said: "Get ye down all from here; and if, as is sure, there comes to you, guidance from me."

Why is it that so many people run around in life saying they have a fear of God? What is the fear they say they feel? If it is something that they feel because of where they were standing in the physical world, then those next to them would feel it too, in the exact same degree. You know yourself that if you choose to express love, fear disappears. It is not an outward fear, but an inner experience because of your leaning in the mind. Exactly like when you think about love, you feel love. The fear of God you say you have does nothing more than broadcast to those enlightened ones around you that you are leaning in the mind in the wrong direction. These fears of God that you say you have are your own fears arising because you are standing in the tribal zone, the tribal self.

Through loving surrendering, God's guidance speaks to you as the small voice of inspiration. You have to raise yourself out of this comfort zone, this tribal self, up into the greater states of awareness where you will truly experience the love of God. Those of you, who dwell within the light, do so because of their own inner expression of true love. True love is a divine expression and there is no fear when Heavenly love is manifest and expressed by you.

When you reside within the light, an expression from those that reside there is different from the expression that comes from the irregularities. When you live in love, you live in God and in God's light, there is no fear, you only find love. One of the great beauties of this physical world is that two people can be in the same place, yet consciously reside at opposite ends of the Law of Polarity. From this, you will realise how God can independently enforce His will according to your record of deeds. Indeed, this world is a school where you must learn to become self-aware. You need not be God fearing when you open your heart in love and follow the guidance of the small voice of loving truth. God turns towards those who listen to the inspiration that comes to them.

Sura 21 Verse 102

*102. Not the slightest sound will they hear of Hell: what their souls
desired, in that will they dwell.*

The irregularities you hear come from the place you call Hell. For
people who turn their back and do not charge headlong into such
whispers, God will forgive their wonderings in the mind. He will
guide them out of the darkness into the light. It is for you to listen
to and follow the wisdom that flows from the light. This will raise
you out of the base matter that surrounds you.

We each belong to a group. From this group we descended into the
physical world from the spiritual. Spirits from your group can be
born in another country, so in your ranting and raging, as you shout
at them, you shout at yourself. A spirit group is a collection of spirits
and they are your spiritual family. Your Earthly family is not
necessarily made up of those from your group because each
spiritual group needs the variety of experiences that the physical
world has to offer to aid its growth.

There is a time in everybody's life when the body eventually
becomes exhausted and the spirit withdraws. The spirit returns to
its home in the hereafter. After a while, the energy of creation and
manifestation draws your spirit's attention to a space. You are able
to enter again, the physical reality and work to amend the record of
your deeds. Your Guardian angel comes to you and asks you if you
would like to return. They show you in advance the life you are
about to undertake on planet Earth. For people who surrender and
choose loving kindness over selfishness, they will eventually pass
beyond the Law of Cause and Effect that creates this space on
Earth, where they reap what they have sown.

We are each a miniature universe of the whole. Within you, you
will find that the tribe puts forth its plan. The greater states put
forth their truth through the evolved self. What you choose plants
itself within the gardens of your inner self where it will grow. If
what you chose is from the tribal zone, it acts like a bully, which

beats back the wisdom of your inner book of light. If you accept what is lighter, what is brighter over the tribal self, the light wins a great battle in the struggle.

Chapter 11: Trust and Truth

There is a point within each of us that goes beyond right and wrong. It goes far beyond culture, traditions, ceremonies or rituals. Look to the part of you that only knows love. That knows no violence. That knows no pain. That knows no anger. It does not judge. It does not indulge in false or irregular desires. It sees the divine expression of God in all things. You know within what you must do to reach this inner place.

We call the place that exists beyond the physical world, the world of spirit. As already mentioned, the masculine energy that was to become one-half of the human race was given the name Adam and the feminine energy was given the name Eve. The inner core essence of Adam is truth. The inner core essence of Eve is trust. In the sight of God all are equal. When God looked on His creation and His creation looked back, a loving energy became the bond that forever unites each of us to God and to each other. We call this bond, love.

As the masculine and feminine energies started to venture out into God's creation, they reflected back to God their gratitude. The two energies integrated, forming a partnership, balancing each other as they explored His universe. As they went out, they eventually grew apart. God said; 'Go forth and multiply'. This is exactly what they did. From the inner depths of Adam there was produced the green light of growth and Eve produced the pink light of fertilisation. This integration or relationship between them produced vibrations giving birth to new spiritual beings. The same process takes place on planet Earth between man and woman but on a smaller scale. Adam has the truth, Eve has the trust, and through a combination of these, when love is expressed, the passageway to God remains open.

As time went by our wonderings took us far from God. God created a suitable world where we descended. Through a birth into physical matter bodies, we are able to turn around the process of wanting to be separate from God. On this world of planet Earth, there are people who remained aware of their divine connection to the afterlife. Other people have yet to find their way. This Earth is like a stop sign and as we congregate on its surface, some people halt the fall, reverse the process and head home. Some people become confused and run around bewildered by all they hear and see, not sure which way to direct their consciousness. Then there are other people who think they are self-sustaining and independent.

Adam's nature is to express truth and accept in truth what is presented to him. Eve's nature is to express trust and accept and express herself according to her inner trust. In our human form, Adam represents the unconscious. Eve is the subconscious self. Your conscious self becomes a place within you where the two forces of light and darkness meet to discuss matters. The result of the meeting between the old you and the new you, is the platform where many matters are resolved.

It is through your leaning in the mind that the world you live in exists. As you surround yourself with the things you create, they restrict or raise your consciousness. What is irregular, forces itself on you. You add to or peel away its degrees of intensity until it sits comfortably within you. Your feelings rise up in defence to protect you from falling. The wisdom within your feelings calls you to the light. As Eve, the subconscious self, places her trust in what she receives. She passes this on to Adam, the unconscious self, who accepts it as truth. This passing from one to the other is symbolic of the apple in *The Bible*. Eve is not responsible for the temptation of Adam in the way taught through the intellect. Neither is Eve any lesser than Adam.

Truth and trust accept all things and reflects it back to you as a vision. As the result begins to manifest and present itself to you, you have to make a choice. The fact that you are always aware of the inner truth and trust shows that God and His angels are ever around you, ever inspiring you. The Law of Freewill choice allows you to listen or discard the information sent to you. As you open the doorway to trust, you enter into the inner core essence of Eve. When you hear the inner truth and follow its course, you have connected to the inner core essence of Adam. As you set sail on the sea towards a land clean and good, put your trust in the truth. As trust re-enters truth in total surrender, this union forms a divine unconditional loving expression.

Reason gives rise to intentions, leading to thought manifestations. Be aware that some of your intellectual ideas can block your inner vision. Does your fear of the truth and trust cause you to create a religion other than the one God established for you? All you believe may be but an image from the build-up of partial truths you have accepted or created for yourself. When you refuse to surrender, your whole self falls into error. When truth and trust unite in love on a decision, God's form appears on the horizon as a light within the garden of your inner self.

If your relationships do not appear to flow in harmony, is it due to an imbalance within? In a relationship, if you do not learn how to share the roles of masculinity and femininity, you will not find the balance. The breakdown of any relationship is because of conflicting masculine and feminine qualities. This can be due to the differences in the expression of energy around each of you. This imbalance shows up in the way you communicate. Your relationships bring out what is within so you can work to release, balance, expand and grow.

People who do not inwardly reflect try to make sense of spiritual stories using their intellect. The intellect, for all its intelligence cannot see very far. It is methodical in its approach to the things before it. Because it has no vision of its own, it cannot fully understand the language of the Heavens so it turns to the world for an interpretation. The inner core essence of trust and truth wants to step forward and help you see what the intellect does not. These inner essences are not in conflict with each other. They speak with loving truth and they trust without fear.

If you do not understand the meaning of love, how are you going to explain it to your children? You will find that every thought you have is an expression of the energy that is within and surrounds you. Become self-empowered and listen to your inner truth as you stand within your own inner centre. As your experiences draw to a close, there is a gathering and presenting of the final ending. The accumulation of active thoughts and pictures within you stirs your feelings or emotions.

The conscious self is the child. At first, the child listens to their parents. As the child gets older, they become more aware of choice. As they begin to amass information about their surroundings, they start to listen, mainly to their own inner dialogue. As they make choices, their inner community begins to have a greater sway on their actions. As the child matures, they become independent of their parents and responsible for their freewill choices as they begin to co-create their own destiny. They begin to see and gradually make a distinction between their darkness and their light. In the conscious self, there is a comfort zone where they store what they learn. Over the years, as the child tries to fit themselves into this comfort zone, conflict within their cognitive process manifests. Out of this conflict a new land appears. Their darkness becomes the tribal self. As the child explores this land and takes up residence, they start to change into what exists within this place. The greater the hold the tribal self has on the child, the deeper they eventually sink into self-pity and victim mode. The evolved self grows through a loving surrender. If the child follows the advice that flows from this centre, they will find their own true centre.

Let us go deeper into the never-ending depths in the expression of feelings and the creative inner self. Doing so will help you to realise how the expression of love and meditation helps you fulfil your life's work on Earth. The masculine is the giver associated with being creative and logical. You move around your own polarity, passing through each phase like the waxing and waning of the moon. The feminine likes to receive, to think. Her reference to life is mainly through what is happening within her emotions or feelings. The feminine learns to make a decision and trusts in her feelings or emotions as she listens to her intuition. The masculine likes to see mainly through the eyes of logic and creativity. However, these are both interchangeable and governed by degrees. For your spiritual self to express itself fully it has to find a balance between its femininity and masculinity. You create according to what you give and receive. Without a balance, imbalance in the receiving and giving process occurs. To help the development of these attributes, it is good for the female and the male to come together. As you and they grow in feelings of love, wisdom presides because they work on what is surfacing for the benefit of the relationship. The wisdom that is born out of the relationship between truth and trust creates gardens full of beauty.

The Spiritual Law of Cause and Effect, and the Spiritual Law of Attraction are laws set up to aid each one of us. With this knowledge, think about the following information, using it to create a better life. As you learn to understand the relationship between the feminine and masculine, the unconscious, the subconscious and the conscious self, your awareness about the co-creating manifesting process will become clear. You can see the Adam and the Eve, the truth and the trust, as they surround every action and reaction in your life. Through the expression of love, you are able to evolve and awaken the godly qualities that are innate within you. In your meditations, as you purposefully create, according to the intensity of your willpower, you can materialise or dematerialise the things surrounding you.

The rivers of inspiration that flow through your land play a part in the process of creation that leads to a manifestation. The essence of this creative part of you does not judge but, allows you to direct and use its power in every way you please. As you express love, your godly qualities grow, giving you the appearance of royalty.

All that manifests in your life comes from yourself. If you were not part creator of your destiny, why do you reap all you sow? You must have created something that activated the Law of Cause and Effect. The question is: What? There would be no need for God's judgement about what you do if another person was responsible. God's laws watch over all things created and are perfect in apportioning and guidance. These laws are like a set of procedures acting as a framework or mirror, granting each of us our merit, according to our deeds. However, there is among many people, a lacking in the understanding of the Spiritual Laws working in their lives. Instead of the laws elevating them, they are using them to weigh themselves down. Through these laws, you are able to inspirationally manifest and clothe that manifestation in a new material form. You could say that this book is a new manifestation. It started out as a thought, but now it is here. Alternatively, you can attract to yourself from among the things already here in the physical world. You are reading what is here because you attracted this book to yourself. It came to you because you are ready. Knowing this should help you to understand you are on the receiving end of all your own doings. You are here for the benefit of yourself and you are a co-creator of your destiny.

Once the thoughts have gathered in the conscious self and they have become complete as a vision, you either accept or reject them. Once the subconscious has looked at the created activity, similar or previous events stored within your immediate record steps forward, through memory recall. You piece together the current and the previous memories. As you measure one against the other, it is here that matters are determined. It is not how much you remember - it is how deeply you remember. As you formulate a conclusion and create a new vision from the gathered information, you modify your memory-related perception, according to the leaning in your mind. Both sides of your polarity step forward and present before you a vision to win your approval.

As your manifestation comes into view within your mind, it sits in time and space waiting to be clothed in physical matter as lessons of experience. Alternatively, it is stored and waits for you in the hereafter. During this process, your consciousness activates your feelings. As you expand, what you create in error is subdued or it pushes on through to establishing itself in the land. God gave us this ability to create. He set up the Spiritual Laws to govern our activity. However, many of us take what God has given and ignore our spiritual origin and duty. Use this affirmation to help you create better choices.

From my heart do I create.
In trust, truth and love there are no mistakes.
Perfect my vision that I might see.
And create with love my spiritual destiny.

By consciously knowing how you create your reality, you will come to know how you can un-create and then recreate anew. As there is a need for you to grow, your inner loving community will co-operate and inspire you, co-creating events in your life to help you clear away deeply buried scenarios that block your free-flowing ability to express unconditional love. When you meditate, as you release blockages of energy, this saves you going through the physical experience your inner self manifests to release it and heal you. The experiences that manifest in your life do so according to God's divine plan. It is for you to listen, create and seek the wisdom to help you understand your experiences. Every experience you go through offers within itself learning, cleansing and healing for you. Working with the inner core essences of truth and trust, you put right the record of your deeds. Whatever experiences you seek to be a part of, getting caught up in the middle may not be the best thing for you. In loving surrender, you pass right by such matters, while other people stop and stare. While in the middle of what you perceive to be a self-sabotaging experience, learn to create according to your greatest love, truth and trust, working to dissolve the manifest error that grieves you. When you think about something, you bring what was sleeping to life. Giving birth to ideas, you then fill its interior. As you oversee what manifests, you can modify what you see. All this takes place within you, for you are the trust and the truth, the Adam and the Eve. You oversee all things that happen in your world. Your perception of the world is a result of your Adam and your Eve coming together. You have a choice to reject or accept, what manifests within and around you. You can give life too or withdraw life from any of the scenarios within your world. You give birth to new ideas and watch them grow. Let these new births transform you from darkness into light.

Each of us has come to this world for the same reason. We are here to enlighten ourselves. The closest word we have to understanding ourselves in relation to God is spirit. This part of us is beyond everything we physically see. All things are but an expression of spirit. We are divine conscious beings who have come into this world of learning to raise our consciousness through experience. We all know there is one overall God. His divine qualities exist within us as small seeds. It is up to each of us how we grow and develop them. As we rise from sleep, our godly qualities expand by command. Think about the ninety-nine names of God and then look to your own self. As you oversee all that manifests within your world, you can apply the majority of the ninety-nine names of God to yourself. The names show up as beautiful seeds of wisdom within the garden of your inner self. They sit there waiting for you to cherish them to full growth. You can choose to acknowledge the names or you can choose not to acknowledge them. As your godly qualities become one expression of love, you evolve beyond the needs of the physical reality.

As we grow, the light of our inner self expands. The essence of our inner light is love. When we express love, it energises us on every level. It is for you as a creative being of spirit to initiate the changes on planet Earth. A quick reminder about one of the first sentences from *The Quran* used in this book; *'That there will be no change until we change what is within our souls'* Sura 13 Verse 11. Irregularities want to oppress your loving freedom of expression because they know where there is love and a light, they cannot exist.

All that is within develops a need to express itself. What you call a trauma is a life force of traumatic visions and memories you yourself have experienced, created or enacted at some time during your existence. These traumas create dark spots within you. A trauma can lay hidden within you for a long time. We can keep adding to it, building layer on layer until it is so deeply buried within that we lose sight of it. For example, here is a story about someone going through a very difficult time. The vision received through inspiration showed the event took place around 400 years ago. It was a traumatic event in her life. The emotional turmoil she suffered during the enactment of an irregular activity left a horrific imprint on her inner self. Her story is that, as she stood waiting for someone on the outskirts of a town on the bend of a river, next to some bushes, someone viciously attacked her. The situation caused her much upset and emotional disorientation. Because of the social interactions of the time, her only way of dealing with what had happened to her was to suppress the whole matter, as it was not something to ever speak about. So, she could release the negative emotion of the trauma and restore balance and heal herself, certain emotional conditions from the past event had to re-manifest in her present life. As a way of helping her through it this time around, the energy of the trauma came to the surface in a safe environment where the social conditions around her were more open, loving, and caring. As the release of the trauma manifested, it threw her into disorientation as it had done all those years ago. It was only through the loving care of her sister and family members that she emerged on the other side of the experience to carry on with her life.

The mind allows you to see, in a safe environment, the content of your spiritual self. Your body's function is to balance your spiritual energy in a way that helps you create and develop the divine light within you into a full flame.

You can learn to know what is going on within your own body through feelings and visualisation. Listen to your inner truth and put your trust in what you see in the mind. As you sense matters within the physical body, you can send loving thoughts to the affected area you perceive needs a healing. During meditation, let yourself be open enough to detect problems someone else is having within their physical body, using your body as a mirror. By attuning yourself, you can feel something of their spiritual condition. Create a light of healing and see it surrounding them. As their inner light grows, they will start their own healing process.

Try not to see other people's actions, believing those actions are responsible for the way you feel. They too are acting out what they have accepted as truth. They are in your life and you are in their life. The way you help them is according to the inner direction you face. Teach them that you are not in their life to create duality. When you treat them with love, every time they see you, they will associate loving feelings towards you, helping you to heal. Repeat this affirmation to heal your heart.

> *Light and love within my heart*
> *Help me make a brand-new start.*
> *Every day will bring about*
> *A gentle healing of my heart.*

The more you listen to the voice of the greater truth, the clearer it will become manifest. Through your inner dialogue with the truth, you will receive your proof and evidence of its wisdom. The truth and the trust walks hand-in-hand with you through all your Earthly experiences. They work together as your advisor, counsellor, coach, administrator and most of all, your true friend. They will help you in every task you are involved. If the loving voice of your angel says; 'Go this way instead of that way', listen and follow their counsel. This loving voice will put your safety first. The one who is speaking to you knows more than you do. This voice knows what is before you and what went on behind you. It knows what is around the corner before you get there. This inner voice holds your true life's purpose within its heart centre.

A point of remembrance is that all things have a polarity. Part of your self-development is about you learning to self-manage your whole self as you work to raise yourself up into the light. You can do this by activating your feelings and letting them become your door to inspiration and guidance. Through your negative emotions, you get to know the base matter into which you were born. Through your feelings and intuition, you get to raise yourself into the light. People who listen to their feelings and follow the wisdom have indeed heard the calling that comes through their evolved self.

Love is not a force that is intellectually easy to understand. When someone does not fulfil your list of expectations, centre yourself within your heart and look again. Maybe you are looking according to your negative emotional need to have a list. However, do not forget to look and see what wisdom has to offer. When the tribal self sends forth its portion, your memory recall and desires adds to it. This creates an increase in the load you carry. The intellect, like a fishing net, it examines and extracts information from the river. Which river do you choose? One river is salty and bitter, the other river is sweet and fragrant. The result shows up within the conscious self. What you see or hear plants itself in the garden of your inner self. As you explore the information, you peel back its layers or add to them. The thoughts and images become a part of the land where you dwell. In a land that is clean and good flows a river of love. As you sail along your chosen course, will you flow with a favourable wind, extracting good things to eat?

The following laws mean the same, however, they are expressed in a different way. For example, the deeds that your hands have sent forth and the reaping of what you have sown mean the same. The Law of Equality referred to in *Sura 2 Verses 178, 179 and 194*. It is also expressed as an eye for an eye and a tooth for a tooth as in *Sura 5 Verse 48*.

As well as: 'You reap what you sow'; there is also 'As you think, so shall it be'; and 'What your hands have sent forth'. These sayings are not idle chatter. When you explore such expressions, you see within them a greater meaning. They are Spiritual Laws. *The Quran* talks about equality. All life is precious and governed by the Spiritual Law of Equality. To see someone lesser than you, it shows where you need to work on yourself. You are not viewing life from your higher self if you believe you are better than someone else.

You have to realise that you are the creator of your own experiences within the pre-destined landmarks set out in your life. You will continue to accumulate through the Law of Cause and Effect and the Law of Attraction, reaping what you have sown. You have an exact experience according to what your hands have sent forth. Your goal in life should be to express feelings of love. During the experience, the love that flows from you, you should not have any conditions attached to it. Unfortunately, in the physical world, love is not as measurable as the gathering of material gains.

If you sit at home and do nothing, is it anybody's fault? God's greatest gift to you is life. Here on planet Earth, you are free to create. In your choice, do you choose to create light or do you choose to create the darkness? The light and love within you are not there for you to let it lie dormant. Dwelling within the base matter into which you are born is not striving in the way of God. You have to raise yourself out of the conditions that surround you. As the way opens before you, you gather up the harvested seeds of wisdom. They grow to become your foundation. Let self-restraint help you in your endeavours. All that is within you is there for you to use in one way or another. On your journey, God and the angels arrive at the appointed time and place but there is no sign of you ever having entered the sacred mosque. Is it that you have not understood the meaning of surrender? When pollution fills the river that flows through the land, your mind fills with false desires and empty promises. Does your tribal self say; 'I will make you promises, yet I will not keep them?' Ask yourself, who it is you are imitating in behaviour and becoming likened too? Are you taking on the expression of the ninety-nine names of God? Alternatively, are you representing the tribe and its false desires? Refer to *Sura 14 Verses 22-24* for clarification.

Chapter 12: Seeking God's Face

Sura 3 Verse 139
139. So lose not heart, nor fall into despair: for ye must gain mastery if ye are true in faith.

The inner light you see during meditation is the light of God. From this light come the seeds of truth. They plant themselves within your inner garden. However, to enter the light you must strive hard against your own irregularities. Using the wisdom within the seeds of truth, seek inspirational guidance. Through the light, you find *Janna* (Heaven). The small flickers you see in meditation are the tips of the bright beauty of Heaven. Once your vision of this light is complete, you will be able to step into it at any time.

Sura 57 Verse 28
28. He will provide for you a light by which ye shall walk (straight in your path).

Sura 2 Verse 272
272. Ye shall only do so seeking the 'Face' of God.

The word 'Earth' in *The Quran* is sometimes metaphorical for the mind. In Chapter 18: Your Inner Truth, we look at *Sura 6 Verse 1,* which talks about God making the darkness and the light. In *Sura 24 Verse 35,* God is the light of the Heavens and the Earth. When you put the two verses together, the information gives you a greater picture. Not only did God make the darkness and the light. He is both, however, He calls you to the light. Your vision will now tell you that God is in the light of the Heavens. You see this light with your mind's eye. This light creates a beautiful Heaven and a place of sanctuary for you. Again, we can see here how meditation benefits you as you go in search of truth. The light you see with the eyes of the inner self during meditation is indeed God's face. The light is God's vehicle so you might know *The Quran* speaks the truth to you. God is the light, however, not the light itself. When this is applied to you, your body is a vehicle for your spirit self. *Sura 2 Verse 272* refers to the light as; *'seeking the face of God'*. Also, read *Sura 6 Verse 52* and *Sura 18 Verse 28*. Your body is an instrument that your spirit uses to perfect itself as it travels on its journey. As you meditate and travel the inner *hajj,* you see the light using your inner spiritual vision. Let the light radiate all around you. It is here that you become aware and know that God is always with you. God is present in your life. He is not in some far distant box at the other end of His creation. Your physical body is, for you, the house where God's sanctuary sits, suspended in time and space. It exists within you that you might visit. This place is the place where God comes to meet you. Does God come to meet and greet you even when there is no trace of you ever having visited your sacred mosque? God is the light of the Heavens and the Earth. You can know God through the light you see. As God presents Himself to you as the light, go within and have a conversation with God. Repeat this affirmation to help you see the truth.

Let the light within me rise.
Let me stand within its calm.
Let its vision become my vision.
Let its love become my love.
Let me keep with what I say.
Let me smile another day.
Let love help me on my way.
Let me be true until the end of days.

You can see God and experience His love through the light. Those who are steadfast, one day their awareness of God's presence will be forever present with them. The *'Good ye give'* is the spreading of God's love and light to other people. God has created each of us on this patterning. As you seek to draw closer to the light, your spiritual self will fill with its radiance. It is in this understanding that you will begin to know that God is within you and He will reveal Himself to you as the light. To see the light, create a state of loving kindness during your meditations. You start your journey having entered the base matter of your portioned amount. You must raise yourself up from this place, using your experiences as building blocks. You will eventually reach your true centre and place of sanctuary. It is within the centre of light that you will recognise the true form of all things. Those who see and follow the light must one day meet the one who is shining that light. When you see and feel the love of the light, you will know it is God's light because of what comes from it. Those who have never seen the inner light believe it to be something produced by the electrical circuits of the body. They believe this for a number of reasons.

Four Reasons of Unbelief

1. They have not seen the light for themselves.

2. Their intellect tells them it is something created by the mind.

3. Their irregularities hold such sway over them that it blocks their view and understanding of the light.

4. They are distracted by the ways of the world.

Your mind is the door to your conscious self. Through it, you choose between the darkness and the light. You cannot wait for science to provide you with answers because of your doubts. Those who say you cannot see God's face do so because they have convinced themselves it is impossible. Yet The Quran tells you to seek the home of the hereafter. That we should seek the face of God. When you attach yourself to and fit yourself into the historical beliefs of those around you, you will feel doubts, stresses and strains. However, your inner self suggests the truth in a bid that you might listen. We are all individuals and we will never fit exactly into someone else's belief system. In life, the only truth you will ever feel comfortable following is within yourself.

Sura 2 Verse 257
257. God is the protector of those who have faith: From the depths of darkness He will lead them forth into light.

There is a general belief in the existence of Hell and Heaven. *Sura 34 Verse 18* says that not only was Heaven and Earth created but there are cities at prominent positions. Expanding on this further is to know that there are cities in the afterlife. These are located in the various states of Heaven. Touching on this later, you will see that Heaven and Hell are states of mind. There are seven major levels or planes of existence around each world. Each of these planes has within it dimensions, or worlds within worlds, and within these places are cities at prominent positions. Your consciousness can reach out and enter these places as you spiritually develop. However, you must fulfil certain conditions within yourself before you can freely enter. For example, the place called *Bakka*, referred to in *Sura 3 Verse 96*. As a quick reminder, there are places beyond what you call Heaven. In *Sura 55 Verse 33*, it refers to zones beyond the heavens, the beginning of pure spirit.

To help you know your true self, you need to realise that the physical body is but one of numerous bodies you have. As well as the physical body, you have spiritual bodies, each one like an overcoat. The one you are most familiar with is the physical body, then you have the etheric, followed by the astral body, followed by feelings, mental and higher-mental bodies and then, the soul. Beyond this is your spiritual self. You use these duplicate bodies like avatars, in that you are able to transfer a greater part of your consciousness into one of these bodies and use it as a vehicle. As you raise your consciousness, these bodies become one body of spiritual light and love. God uses spiritual energy as His vehicle. Through this energy, He produces a light that guides you out of the darkness. In *The Quran,* it refers to our spiritual bodies as ships we use for sailing. To break them down in a little more detail they include: physical and emotional; etheric and wellbeing; astral and dreams; feelings and awareness; mental and inspiration; higher mental and visions; soul and spiritual self; and the life hereafter. You will notice that one of your bodies is a body of feelings. It has a greater state of awareness than the physical and emotional body.

When you help someone to overcome their emotional difficulties, you are helping them to transform their emotions into light. When you transformed your emotions from sadness into feelings of happiness, you did not lose anything. You moved yourself out of one state and into another. When raised you say; 'I feel better now'. You are using the word 'feel' associated with your feelings. When you feel something, you are not using the confliction forces of your emotional self. Alternatively, you say; 'That situation has hurt my feelings'. The vision through your feelings is far greater than your emotional vision. Feelings are in degrees closer to truth. Learn to put your feelings before your emotions. By transforming your emotions, you will become more than you were. You will still be you but you will be a stronger, confident, happier, healthier you, more able to be of service to other people.

Be aware that many Earth lessons are small. However, you will find every so often, you come across a lesson that knocks you sideways. These experiences are spiritual blessings. Those who make the experiences work for them receive all the help they need to push on through to the other side. Your life is a journey that you cannot avoid because your spiritual self knows what is best and proceeds to produce experiences accordingly.

God does not raise you up blind. Do you not bother to listen and develop the godly qualities bestowed on you? In your choices, are your only concerns about the goings on in the material world and did you leave alone your godly qualities that enhance your loving spiritual nature? If you looked in the wrong direction and lost your vision of truth, you know you will one-day return to the hereafter. How can you expect to see clearly in the afterlife if you do not learn how to develop your spiritual vision or any of the other godly qualities bestowed on you?

How can you develop the beautiful godly qualities of your spiritual self? First, learn to love, and then surrender. When the practice of *muraqabah* is applied, you are truly on your way to seeking the face of God. The practice of *muraqabah* allows you to enter the essence of who you are and directly work to enhance God's gift. As you start the inner journey of self-discovery, the first person you will come across is yourself. The person you believe yourself to be will appear to you as an expression of defence mechanisms. The outer person you think is you, will turn out to be but the feedback you get from other people as you interact with them. Your outer expression is according to the perceptions and opinions you think other people have of you. Because of the doubts you feel, you invent a character you believe is strong enough to defend you. You are a light of the spiritual, consciousness that exists everywhere. All that stands between you and an awareness of the spiritual life force is this invented shadow of yourself. Travel to the world of light and love and see what awaits you. The old emotional 'you' disappears and the new 'you' will emerge. Your inner truth and trust strengthen the ideas that all things are in the hands of God. You recognise the workings of the Spiritual Laws around you as God's plan unravels.

Hold your focus within your heart centre. Let love pour forth to become the fire you kindled. It has a magical way of interacting and restoring harmony and balance where there is imbalance. The origins of this loving energy formed out of the relationship forged between God and His creation. We are able to fill ourselves with this loving energy. In this physical world, only when enough of loves substance has accumulated within you, will you consciously be aware of the spiritual unification of all of humanity. Our craving for love is an inner need to connect to the greater part of who we really are. However, instead of expressing this divine inner essence, we hide inside what we create out of conjecture, afraid to look at our own inner beauty.

Allow yourself to meditate and go back in time to when you first came into existence. God created you from energy. You fill yourself with love, sound, and light. Work to restore yourself to your former beauty. Look for the light. Hear the perfectly-sounding musical note. Kindle the fire, the flame, the light of God within your own self. By your own will, you must bring yourself back into harmony and balance with the natural flow and order of God's divine expression of love.

Let the energy, sound and light produced in the beginning emanate from you. Let it be rich in colour and filled with love. Lights, colours, sounds and vibrations are all expressions of the spiritual self. The sounds and melodies of words that come to your mind are an accumulation of what flows through you. Let the music that comes to you, and from you, be beautiful in its address to other people. Speak to their heart centre, as you would have them speak to yours. Repeat this affirmation to connect with your truth.

I call on truth to guide me along.
I will listen to the whispering angels love song.
In silence they come, planting gifts in my soul.
I listen to their wisdom as it unfolds.

Chapter 13: The Book of Wisdom and Guidance

Reasoning is a flowing river. Its opposition is stubbornness. When you listen to reason, you enter its vibration, extracting the wisdom contained therein. This allows you to flow with a more favourable wind. It sets you on the pathway that leads you to knowledge. Stubbornness will limit your growth because it stops you from seeing beyond what the possibility has to offer. If something is good for you, love shines a light on it to help you see with a greater vision.

What if the thoughts and images that come to you were not from the source you believed? What if all you believed was invented by the expressions of emotional logic, false desire and irregularity? Do not be fooled into thinking you are wise, when all you are using are intellectual evaluations constructed according to physical matter, its movement and expression. Because you have been told something, which was reinforced by other people, it does not make it true. In *Sura 6 Verse 116,* it refers to how majority thinking does not make it right. Your emotional logic excites you into constructing an image before the face of God. The dense crowd stands with its back to God trying to block your view of the light. You see the images they send forth as pursuable delights and you swerve. Be aware of the partners that set themselves up as gods within you. You want to believe they are your friends as they move into your home and become your living partners. However, they are not.

As you learn to work with your feelings, the love energy you feel does not make things complicated. Love is a subtle energy. It appears on the screen of the mind as many different bright and beautiful colours. There is no violence in the land filled with love. When there is too much intellectual, analytical and logical thinking, the search for God becomes complicated. The search for God is quite simple really; surrender yourself to your feelings of love. Surrender and seek to balance weight with justice. A good business plan is one that takes care of its workers and customers. A good life plan is one that takes care of all the people of the world. Repeat this affirmation to help connect with your wisdom.

Behind wisdom is a power.
Arise within me, wake.
I enter the presence of its might.
As it guides me to the light.

In Sura 2 Verses 19-20, God sends to the unbelievers' rain-laden clouds from the sky. Within them are zones of darkness, thunder and lightning. In the darkness is irregular activity. Those who lean in the mind towards the darkness hear the thunder as it fills their consciousness. The lightning is the energy created as a warning to the unbelievers. There are people who do not care for the light and the wisdom from the Heavens, preferring to live in the darkness. They pretend not to hear the words of wisdom that are sent to their mind. When they step on the middle pathway and the light suggests something, doubt enters and fills their mind. When the light suggests something to the irregularities, the irregularities stare back in horror and disgust. The light raises you up into the Heavens. If God so willed, He could take away your ability to know that there exists within you a polarity. What would happen if you could not distinguish between the light and darkness? What if the angels called to you from within and you did not hear them? Without guidance, where would you find yourself? Do not reject the help that comes to you in case, one day, that help hides itself from you. *Sura 25 Verse 53* is letting you know it is all about which river you drink your fill and a partition between the light and the darkness. Strive hard to cross the barrier from the darkness into the light.

When you choose to let irregular energy fill you it creates a state of being that is out of harmony. When you draw too heavily on this force, its vibrations dim your inner light. The beautiful words of wisdom, accompanied by light, disperse irregular energy. People who find the light within their inner self too bright, do so because of the weight of their irregularities. As you pursue the light, each time you see and enter its surroundings it fills you with blessing. It leaves a piece of itself in you, making you lighter and brighter. As you become filled, you will be able to hold yourself within its radiance for a longer period as you work to cleanse your spiritual self. Focus and strive, pushing yourself with determination through the degrees. Fill your inner self with love, expanding the light to all the people you know, sharing with them your inner love. Know that those you have sent loving thoughts to receive all you send as you bring Heaven to planet Earth. Remember you are a channel for the love and light of God. Let it flow through you and do not put into it irregularities. Use this affirmation to connect with your inner light.

Words of wisdom, Oh light that is bright.
Let me enter into light.
The rain upon my heart doth fall.
God's face appears within me.

Once you have seen or stood in the presence of God's light, it becomes no more a myth but a reality. This time you received help but you must learn to hold your conscious steady. The movement of energy, the seeing of the light and the energy that comes from the light are proof for you about the existence of the greater conscious states of awareness. When darkness surrounds you and you find it difficult to reach the light, remember the times that you were not restricted. You must raise the foundations of your inner self from its lowest degrees. Focus yourself, drawing on your thinking, feelings and willpower. Consistency, steadfastness, firmness and self-control are qualities within you to help you on your journey. The body is a vehicle for the spiritual 'you'. As you work to kindle the light of your inner self, your godly qualities become lighter, brighter and stronger.

Sura 5 Verse 46
46. But why do they come to thee for decision, when they have (their own) laws before them?

As you relate the verses of *The Quran* to you and your journey, what are the laws you have before you? Every thought that enters your mind is from the land where you live. The Spiritual Laws surround you, reacting to the things you create within yourself. What may sometimes appear as chaos is no more than an enactment of the Spiritual Laws unfolding. They move and impress on each of us according to the record of our deeds. We live our lives, making our daily decisions between and within the circumference of the laws. However, with the additional thought processes that we add, we feel the extra weight. The reality is that your record of deeds is not as greater burden as you believe. The additional manifest thoughts you add cause an increase in the load you carry. It is impossible to escape the laws because you are the laws and the laws are you. What you can do is work with, expand and transform your awareness of how best to work with them. They are there to guide you and produce for you your experiences. Work to change the balance of your inner self. In the end, the truth will overcome the untruth. The fate of yourself really does exist in your own hands.

What is here is but a small stepping-stone. Eventually, you will move beyond the need for such ideas. What is here is but a seed. It is for you to harvest and grow the seeds with love. As you transcend the thoughts and ideas that exist within you, there will be an establishment of new feelings of awareness and understanding. This manifests within you as an abundance of new possibilities. Imagine meeting a completely new set of friends who have your best interest in their heart centres. You will find, you adjust and change your behaviour and perception according to these new friends. You no longer need some of your previous defence mechanisms. As you reinvent yourself, you create and build a smoother journey for your future lives. Continue to work and transform the foundation of your inner self. Use your experiences and allow development and change to take place. All ideas outlive their usefulness within the consciousness of each of us. You do not live according to the ideas you had five or ten years ago. We are always creating new ideas and moving on. The whole aim of life is to help us grow and become more than we were. You cannot remain hidden in the base matter of the tribal self, thinking you are out of reach from change. God will bring your true self out. When it is time for us to experience a certain lesson, the Spiritual Laws create and manifest the conditions and we enter the experience.

What makes you think and act the way you do? You are acting according to the thoughts you manifest as the laws impress on you according to your deeds. The truth does not change. However, the way you perceive truth in your life changes. Some of the things that pass through your mind are but echoes and revelations of what you believed the last time you cycled through life. As you reflect in the mind, the Spiritual Law of Cause and Effect and the reaping of what you have sown surround you. To help decide how you direct your life, moral codes of conduct within your soul influence your decisions.

You will find bees nurture other bees to do a specific job. This ensures the survival of the hive, allowing its inhabitants to flourish. The laws that impress on you and direct your existence do so as you must reap what you have sown. Be of those who are wise and strive. The laws allow manifestations to appear as a part of God's divine plan. In them, you delight yourself as you experience your Earthly life. All that is, must happen and God's plan does not fault for a moment.

You live within the framework of a specific light vibration that plays a part in the guidance you receive. The work you choose, the hobbies you enjoy are but loving desires that give you delightful desirable feelings. The things that you enjoy bring light into your inner self. They cause your garden to flourish and grow. The Spiritual Laws are always at work, unfolding as you unfold. Think of your life unfolding like a book, each day a new page and on your birthday a new chapter. Repeat this affirmation to continue your growth.

The spiritual laws surrounding me in life
Are there to help me grow.
Each step I take returns to me.
Tread carefully my soul.

The world is a mixture of people at different stages on their spiritual development. For this reason, there are many interpretations of what is truth. God's laws are perfect and all that reaches you is perfect. There is only one truth but there are many perceptions and according to the placement of your consciousness is according to your view. If one part of a group of people suppresses inspiration, the peoples of the other part will not suppress it. Alternatively, is the truth being taken from you and given to a new people? Do not be too quick to believe in self-glory, separatism and conjecture.

God's throne of authority surrounds all. His words are your words, your words are His words. Do not give yourself completely to another person; neither should you try to fit other people into the laws according to the way they are manifesting for you. It is for each of us to make our own mind up about what is and is not acceptable, necessary or possible. Inspiration balances each of us. When you close the doors of love, you tilt the balance. As you express love, the laws that surround you expand your breast. With the development of your feelings, you can look ahead and feel safe travelling down that road.

Through sharing, you will be better prepared to hear what the angels have to say. Through surrendering and sharing, you learn to unify your consciousness with those who watch over you. They will work with you, forming bonds of friendship. They will extend their energy as you extend yours, joining you through the heart centre. If you are always finding yourself in conflict, how can you expect to find unity with God and His angels? Repeat this affirmation to connect with your truth and trust.

Truth will bring about a change
And my destiny be re-arranged.
Trust will follow as it should
To carry me towards the good.

God gives you the responsibility for your own journey by telling you the way is open as in *Sura 5 Verse 51* and He will not stop anybody from having access. However, there are requirements and conditions that you must internally fulfil. One word is all you need to know: Love. Be clear about what you know. What does the word love mean to you? Do not hide from the questions that arise within. Life is full of possibilities and realities that you have yet to discover. The questions you are afraid to ask could be your own fear of the truth and the changes you have to make. Do not let this shadow of yourself rule your life. Overcome your fears and take the steps that will free you. What you call change will result in an expansion of the light of your inner self. You will have to one day expand and go beyond what you believe yourself to be. You cannot stop learning. Events will come into your life that will teach you a lesson. Even if you were the only person on this whole planet, something would happen that will cause you to think and see things in a different light.

Our fears may be a fear of leaving the safety of community thinking. Are their opinions so much more important than the truth within you? The way to reach the garden of truth is through the acceptance of truthful thoughts. Think or imagine what it would be like or what would happen if we all refused our responsibilities to bring the inner truth forward. Do not wait, get on with what you are supposed to do. If you do not, you will find yourself and your vision ruffled by someone else doing what you refused. Let the inspiration that comes to you through the evolved self, guide you. Listen to the best construction on the options that enter your mind. If you believe in the tribe, you will continue to struggle until you surrender yourself in love.

Do not let anybody tell you it is impossible to see the light of God. His light is the light of your inner self. The light is also with those who say they do not believe. Each person is capable of reaching out and living within the light. Loving expressions manifest within each person. Where there is love, God's light shines. God gives freely to both male and female. He does not turn away because of religious orientation or country of origin. Let these words uproot the falsehoods and disperse them long enough for you to see. As you absorb and integrate the incoming information, you start to build a new foundation of thought. It is for you to find your own way. If need be, develop your own ways of understanding the truth if you are not satisfied with the interpretation or ideas that are presented to you.

When doubters enter the station of the tribal self, what is there surrounds, constricts and hems them in. They say; 'God is our judge and jury'. Why are they joining the tribal self and acting as if they are the judge, jury and executioner of those they believe to be wrong? They build their knowledge from a foundation of fear, false and self-desires, partial truth and suspicious conjecture. All that is in opposition to God must vanish. What is in opposition to God has made a choice not to surrender itself. If it had surrendered to the truth, it would not set itself up as god and make judgements about other people. God is quite able of carrying out His tasks.

There has and will always be people who have not immersed themselves totally in the worlds they visit. They remain aware, holding and maintaining an inner connection to the Heavens. They are the people who do not ignore the small voice of wisdom within themselves. They recognise the guidance from the angels. They hear and see what other people pass by as their awareness detects the presence of the afterlife. The spiritual harvest is indeed different from the material harvest.

Here is the breakdown of *Sura 7 Verse 57*. It will be provided in sections, followed by its metaphorical explanation. Also, read verse 58.

'It is He who sendeth the winds like heralds of glad tidings going before His mercy.'

God sends the Prophets and Messengers, represented here by the word: *'winds'*. The words: *'sendeth winds like heralds'* meaning *'sending forth multiples of'*, *'clusters of'*, or *'groups of'*. They are like a breeze of fresh air in the life of those in search of God's truth. These enlightened beings bring comfort to those in need of reassurance. As a part of God's plan, He creates spaces where He allows His prophets and messengers of truth to enter the physical reality. The words they speak reach every land and every people, giving guidance, showing and explaining to humanity the best way to strive.

'When they have carried the heavy-laden clouds, we drive them to a land that is dead, make rain to descend thereon.'

'The heavy-laden clouds' represent the spiritual wisdom the prophets and messengers of God have gathered. It is in their enlightened awareness that they carry God's wisdom. Their understanding covers a wide range of knowledge about the spiritual and physical realms. They come to the world and must relearn and raise the foundation of their inner self back into the light. Not all those who are messengers are born spiritually enlightened. They have to work hard to raise their consciousness. People who become messengers are tossed about in the world. Their task is to learn how to direct their consciousness and sail their ship. Their remembrance is but a flicker that causes them to ask questions and search for answers. The rain that falls on them revitalises their inner light. Thus, they gain in spiritual wisdom and understanding. They send forth their light and it returns fully charged with wisdom. They draw from the heavy-laden cloud of wisdom or the accumulated light of

their inner self. Their destiny brings them into contact with those waiting to awaken.

' ... and produce every kind of harvest therewith'

As the light grows within, their awareness expands. You have a choice as to which harvest directs your life. As you listen to the inner voice, if you follow the one that speaks through the light, you are destined to become aware of your divine spiritual self. Your spiritual awakening takes you down a new road. There are many jobs carried out by these spiritually awakened individuals. There is a common expression, which is love. There is a devotion to prayer and meditation. All of them are teachers and manifesters. Each travels their pathways gradually awakening to the life of the hereafter. As they surrender, other godly qualities within them activate and spring up, thus they harvest the seeds of a new crop. You do indeed become the cherisher of a beautiful new garden. All that you learn, you carry over to the next life.

'... thus shall we raise up the dead: perchance ye may remember.'

As we each share the message from our inner truth, more of humanity will become aware of their divine connection to the afterlife. *Sura 16 Verse 70* and *Sura 70 Verse 39* explains: Having known much, each of us is returned to the base matter we know. During the early stage of our journey, we are temporarily spiritually dazed and must relearn spiritual knowledge and understandings. As they regain a foothold back on the spiritual ladder, they are soon on their way back to all that is good. They are raised in a new creation, to a spiritual station in a variety of ways, from a variety of backgrounds.

The teachings in the Holy books of God are expressed with such delicacy. Each person who studies is able to partake. They see within the verses according to their degree of spiritual awakening. From the first foundation stones of spiritual wisdom to the present day, we have each been coming and going to and from planet Earth, expanding ourselves a little more each time.

Through meditation, as you gather together wisdom, the information settles, firmly planted. Its accumulation brings about stages of resurrection and enlightened awareness. It has been mentioned before how the first couple of times you meditate, you may feel a little strange. You may, at first feel a little fluttery in the stomach area, a little queasy. You are becoming aware of your own energy. For people who strive and remain true, they will quickly increase in awareness. As the winds of inspiration reach the deepest depths of creation, the harvested seeds release a gift for you. Inspirational thoughts can be seen in the minds of all, so reflect within yourself.

As enlightened beings clothe their spiritual experiences into words, other people find in them an understanding that guides them. The wisdom they gather heals their inner self. As the gates of Heaven open allowing people to see its hidden delights, it is a treasured moment of great beauty. You know there is only one God so pay attention, through inspiration you will be taught. Practise this affirmation to seek greater wisdom.

I call on the winds to bring
The clouds of truth to me
And wash my soul in purest light
Which grants me wisdom and insight.
I call on the clouds of trust
To raise my soul up from its sleep.
That I may read and understand.
The wisdom from the promised land.

Strive to reduce unnecessary thoughts. Slowly you awaken to other possibilities. You too can become a light within the world, a place of sanctuary for people who are seeking the face of God. As you help other people, one mightier in wisdom will draw close and help you.

The harvested seeds of wisdom will help you rectify past mistakes. God wants us to strive, to walk the pathway that leads to Him. Do not imagine and take on history, as you believe it to have been. Look forward and reach out to the clouds as they pass you by. The clouds of inspiration will arrive at their stated destination. In love, you will arrive at your stated destination in time to receive.

Express love in your life and reap the benefits. You should not make your belief an extension of someone else's historical conjecture. Your today is an extension of your thoughts of yesterday. Your own inner self is the best reminder about the truth of your history, which goes back far beyond any of the history books. It goes back to when God first created you. After your birth, you sent light out, it returned with a blessing. You sent out light again, it returned with a gift, and you had your first memory recall as you compared one vision with another.

Read *Sura 3 Verses 96-97* and note how another interesting Spiritual Law is the Law of Opposites, which states: *'As above so below'*. There is a place of pilgrimage beyond this world of physical matter. The name of the place in the afterlife you can visit is *Bakka*. Within the afterlife, there is the station of Abraham. Look at the journey within as a spiritual *hajj* where you are able to raise yourself to a higher station. People make pilgrimages to the different shrines and places of worship on Earth. People and all kinds of beings make pilgrimages to the hereafter while still connected to their physical body. They are aware that they have transferred a greater part of their consciousness to one of their spiritual bodies. As you strive forward and reach out, you will perceive the spiritual station of Abraham. Humans and beings in the hereafter come together for spiritual events in the same way there are Earthly gatherings in this world. Take note that *The Quran* talks about *'worlds'* and not only one *'world'*. Your thoughts can limit you from experiencing and knowing about the existence of these other worlds. However, our physical bodies do not limit those beings in the greater states as they come to inspire and help with the evolution of humanity. We get help from beings that have themselves transformed and transcended their planetary evolution. When desires trap you and your vision only points in the direction of this worldly life, you miss so much. You use a very small percentage of your true potential in this physical world. Many things exist alongside of us of which most people have no knowledge. When something is outside of your awareness, the intellect tries to fill in the details. Its assumptions do not give you a true picture. When those in ignorance have fear in their mind, their vision becomes filled with fear. This is projected towards the world around them. They believe that a spiritual knock on their door is something evil. They fail to understand that it happens so that they might know the hereafter is real. Their light becomes dark because of their belief in partial truths.

I call on the greater truth
To raise me up to thee.
To a station far beyond
Irregularity.

Read *Sura 40 Verse 15* and ask yourself: 'Have you ever wondered how spiritually evolved beings communicate across long distances?' Telepathy is a fact to those who have experienced it. You may ask why more people do not experience telepathy if it is a fact. Many people do but they are unaware of it. It would be very difficult for us to last a day if we did not receive telepathic inspiration. What do you think inspiration is? It is the small voice of your angel as he or she speaks to you. They are there, inspiring you. God assigned to you the Law of Freewill, His angels will not tell you what to do, they will only suggest something for your consideration. Before telepathy between the majorities of people is widely experienced, a lift in the consciousness of humanity needs to take place. This is because of the violent thoughts expressed out of fear. God keeps us protected from hearing such irregularity. Refer to *Sura 21 Verse 80*.

You may have come across someone who says they speak to their cat or dog. When you read *The Quran*, you will find a story that talks about conversing with animals. Everything has a spirit, including animals, vegetables and minerals. Those of you who have had an experience of telepathy know that it is a much clearer and direct way of communication. With this kind of communication, you do not only get the sound. You also see and feel the vibrational energy that follows the thought. Even in a place filled with hundreds or thousands of people, you can single out the individual from where the communication came.

At this moment, you may be unaware of any other presence except your own. The prophets came to show us how to work and flow with the Spiritual Laws. That we are immature seeds waiting to open our awareness as the prophets have done. Solomon was one such man. He was able to communicate with the animal kingdom. This awareness exists within you as a little light or an immature seed. It is for you to expand this seed, harvesting it into a full flame.

Sura 27 Verses 18-19, tells the story of the valley of ants. Do not think about your pathway. You could be further along than you believe. Include meditation as a part of your life, you have nothing to lose, only to gain. You may not have been aware of the developments that have been taking place within you, directing you to your moment of spiritual awakening. In that moment, your awareness will expand and illuminate around you. Each experience in your life is a key turning within you, unlocking the door a little more to the mysteries of the Heavens. There will be times when you will feel yourself drawn towards the Heavens. Your spirit's vibrations quicken, raising you to a greater degree of consciousness, elevating you. Protected inside your bubble of light and shyness, your vision becomes small as though you are gazing through binoculars the wrong way, making physical things appear far away. All the experiences in your life are little preparations. You must one day become the captain of your ship. Put all you have been through behind you. Hold yourself steady. You may think you are not ready for the truth, but your angels who hold the truth, know you are ready. You have always been ready. You were born ready. They are waiting to help you rise up from your sleep.

If you re-enter the worldly activities where you left off, you will only be covering ground you have already walked. Let your Guardian angels take you by the hand and remind you of the final stage of your journey home. Learn to feel your way using your thinking, feelings and willpower. Use your reason to make sound judgements and you will find your way. Do not let the fear of change or loss hold you back. Make the necessary changes so you can ride the waves peacefully. Humbleness is not about letting everybody walk all over you. Stand up for your rights. Your humbleness creates an inner world of peace. On a peaceful day, the sun shines bright and love fills the air. The beautiful conditions you create fertilise your inner garden and it flourishes.

Chapter 14: Our True Selves

Sura 20 Verse 50
50. He said: "Our Lord is He who gave to each (created) thing its form and nature and further, gave (it) guidance."

The real 'you' your spiritual self is far greater than the tribe wants you to know about yourself. As long as this tribe exists, it will present to you a belief that this is how it has always been. Not all is well if you believe in 'them and us'. The tribal self is not stable. It shifts its loyalties. As you come to realise your true form, your concept of life as only a physical being will alter. In the next world, free from the restraints of the material body, you are spirit. Once you accept this concept, you will be better able to grasp the idea that spirit is a living, breathing creation of God. You will realise how unique and individual you are, how unique we all are in our own ways, how beautiful we all are in our many colours of radiant light. Those who are awake will wonder how it is possible for us to hate each other in some of the ways we find ourselves hating.

Why do you not try harder to express love? When you recognise your true self, you will realise everyone has this same beauty within. Conflicting duality clouds your vision and limits you. When you are at war with yourself, why ruin people's peace and quiet. Do not allow the war within to overflow into the material world. From a world at war comes the language and expression of war. From a world filled with love comes the language and expression of love. You can do little for those at war whose wish is to try and extinguish the light. All you can do is leave them to their war, for it will eventually exhaust itself.

I am light, you are light.
Joined in love, joined in love.
I am in you, you are in me.
Joined in love, joined in love.

Read *Sura 30 Verse 22*. There are variations in the way truth, partial truth and untruth express themselves. It does not matter which Earthly language you speak. People who strive to reside within the greater degrees of consciousness, speak a language that reflects the state. In every land and every heart, there are words of poetry and music for the inner self. Words of wisdom and beauty exist in all languages. There are also self-sabotaging and self-inflicting thoughts and words that wound and hinder your journey.

Inwardly listen and see with the eyes of your inner self. Clothe God's inspiration in love. You will find the Holy Book of each religion, contains enough wisdom within its scriptures to enlighten you. Words from the heart are words from the heart. They are in line with the divine light of the Heavens. Words of the world are words of the world. They try to disrupt the divine order that God has set up. They are not inspired by divine consciousness. All expressions have their origin in the light. It is the interpretation of the light and the failure to reason in the truth of that light that causes inspiration to become distorted, changed and expressed as something different. As your need for words vanishes, your expression of love is unrestricted by the thought process. Love has great depth, breadth and width. God's love is within you and through love, the divine plan is revealed. Your knowledge of God's divine plan for you depends on your own expression of love.

People who meditate and strive will come across radiant colours as they surrender. They play an important part in an individual's development. Each colour is filled like one of the heavy-laden clouds that carry healing, inspiration and knowledge about God to stated destinations, refer to *Sura 6 Verse 106.* You use these colours to balance your energy vibrations, cleansing yourself of darkness. The visualisation of colour can help heal the physical body, realigning its patterning to bring about balance. You are spirit, and your light is a reflection of the condition of your spirit. When you look at the rainbow in the sky, then look within, you see the alignment of the key colours of your inner being.

The state of your inner self is the first thing you should be contemplating. Are you considerate to other people in thought, words and deeds? Do you see beyond the appearance of people you meet while travelling on planet Earth? Between the creation of all that is Heavenly and all that is of the planet Earth, there is a fine dividing line. All that is Heavenly speaks with words of love. All that is of the tribal self has yet to find its way. From God, love flows to you and from you let love flow to other people. When the time arrives for you to account for your deeds, the colours emerging and swirling around you will reflect your true spiritual condition.

Carefully read *The Quran*. Read it in a language you understand. Let your vision be open to receiving inspiration so that you see the higher wisdom. It is for you to develop your ability to reason things out for yourself. Reach out with your light. You can expand yourself far beyond the limitations your tribal self imposes on you. See other people as you see yourself when in meditation and residing within the highest point of your cycle. We are all ships sailing on the ocean; each of us apportioned an amount by God. The more eloquent your ship, the more gracefully you will sail.

We have touched on this topic here and there but it is worth a few pages to bring it to the front of your mind. An explanation about the Spiritual Law of Polarity is like north and south or hot and cold; between the two extreme points, there are many degrees. Of the Law of Polarity, light is at one end, darkness at the other with many degrees in and between. Each degree like a veil, each degree in the direction of the light takes you closer to God. Each one of us is ever in motion moving between our own points of polarity. Each degree is a land where you can dwell.

Sura 6 Verse 83
83. We raise whom we will degree after degree: For thy Lord is full of wisdom and knowledge.

The lessons we face will eventually bring us to a conclusion that all people are equal and are on a pathway to God. As we are all human beings, we are each able to alter our conscious state of awareness. Your task is to learn what it means to surrender and hold yourself steady in the light. Your inner shadows are a creation from the overuse of the five physical senses, as you direct them towards the physical world. You must show signs of dedication to meditation before you freely pass into the greater states of awareness.

Read *Sura 30 Verse 36* and understand that the thoughts we think become active manifestations in the degrees beyond the physical reality. We send them forth and they become like the winds that blow around the Earth. You can use the thoughts that plague you like a stepping-stone to reach the next level of consciousness. Your determination to succeed will mean you gain mastery over the thoughts that cause you mischief. Instead of living a life dictated by irregularity, you follow only what comes from the highest horizon within yourself. When you create a light that surrounds you, it acts like a coat of armour, it protects you from the violent thoughts of others.

As you cycle around your polarity, you have a great opportunity to expand. You like what you see when you are happy, however, do you really like what you see when you are not? During your inner moment, if you feel yourself begin to drift, there will be a gentle nudge to put you back on track. Practise this affirmation to help you.

The winds of time blow silently
Within my inner world.
Let darkened winds be washed away
To be replaced by the light of God.

The inspiration sent to the messengers of God is the same inspiration that comes to you. When inspiration comes to you, you read the information as thought patterns, feelings and impressions.

Depending on which land you are residing, will depend on how clearly and how deeply the inspiration influences you. At the beginning of this book, there was a question asked: If you were to ask me where this thought or that thought came from, the reply would be; 'Where were you standing when the thought entered your mind?' The answer to that question is: you draw from the river that flows through the garden of the land where you dwell. This river has a source from where it flows. Until you reach a station on high, this source changes like the rotation of the sun and the moon.

The Quran explains that what you see within are signs, refer to *Sura 41 Verse 53.* Remember, in some places in *The Quran* the word *'Earth'* is metaphorical for *'the mind'*. Your consciousness surrounds and sees what springs from the garden of the Earth. Ask to see signs in the inner apartments during your meditations. If you are standing in the right position, with practice and patience, you will learn to see clearly, extracting a great deal from what is impressed on you.

As we have been talking about how we are each able to generate, construct and create, each person's beliefs about the interior of Heaven and Hell will differ. Another related belief is the *Dajjal,* (the Devil, Satan, Iblis, the fallen angel) who refused to bow. What part does this spiritual form play in all of this? This life force still watches over his irregular creation. As you cast your vision over the land in which you dwell, you can clearly see the approach of the army of irregularities. Greater is their fighting among themselves. Do they surround you and persuade you to make a decision in their favour or do you turn your back on them in search of the light? The irregularities eagerly carry you to the door of the tribal self. You enter his world when your leaning in the mind is away from the light. If you do not turn back but instead enter the door to his world, error is sure to manifest.

Sura 2 Verse 112
112. Nay, - Whoever submits his whole self to God and is a doer of good.

Once more, read *Sura 25 Verse 53*, which refers to how there are two energies at work. Without a breaking down process, there can be no renewal. It is for you to reflect on how you self-manage what you know exists within yourself. The result of too much of your energy given to your irregularities causes you to express yourself without due care and attention. For some people, their irregularities may cause them to cut short their cycle on Earth. Truly, a great sadness in what has become manifest.

We will see in the next verse; you reap what you sow in life. Iblis is responsible only for the deeds he commits. Each person is responsible for the deeds they themselves commit. This way, there can be no blame put on another person. You only have yourself to blame. Male and female are indeed equal. The path is open to all. You have to take responsibility. You are the creator of the evil one in your life. You give it the power it craves. You get every opportunity to do what is right. When you think in irregular ways, you give life and power to this form. In a collective consciousness, there grows a collective energy. Irregular thinking feeds this collective energy. It is for us to stop feeding it.

Sura 14 Verse 22
22. Then reproach not me but reproach your own souls.

Sura 38 Verse 82
82. (Iblis) said: "Then by thy power, I will put them all in the wrong."

Life is not about what is happening in the outer world. The outer world is a reflection of an inner expression. You are not responsible for what is going on somewhere else. You are responsible for what you manifest throughout your life. The expression of love will save humanity. When you teach people to love, they live in love. When the inner manifests itself in the outer, the manifesters of discord complain. Your evil works through you using a portion of your energy to keep you from the truth. As the light and the darkness put on a show within the conscious self, which one wins your approval?

From the tribal self, you will look, see and believe as if you know. From this place, a vision of promise will not necessarily manifest. The tribe puts forth the illusion of truth that can cause you to swerve. The tribal self creates many ideas and promises and then fails to deliver. The tribal self has no power of its own and relies on you to feed it. Not even Iblis has any power of his own. He relies on your fears and the power of God as the former couple of verses explain.

All things start out as truth, however, irregularity steps forward and your vision changes. Think what happens over generations. You believe things are true because of the conditioning imposed on you. The lost ones tell you that you have to believe and accept the ideas of past generations. Have you turned your back on the inner truth that comes to you? You know certain things are not true, however, you decide to override your inner wisdom. You should indeed question. Look to the light of your own inner self for the answers. The inner dimensions of your inner self contain the best of truths. Why look for the answers in anyone else? All you need is within. What is in you will eventually manifest itself into your life.

The thoughts within create the interior of our own being. It is through our ability to create that we play a part in the co-creating process. It is through this that we bring into existence the realities of Heaven and Hell. For some people, Hell does not exist because of where their consciousness resides. They move through life in a state of surrender, their hope driving them forward, their love holding them up. Love towards all people will raise your consciousness, placing it within the Heavens. In the hereafter, like will be joined with like. No sound of Hell will you hear as you reside within the light of the Heavens. The sounds of Hell that you hear are irregularities as you lean in the mind and they infiltrate your world.

Read *Sura 21 Verses 101-102* and *Sura 30 Verse 44.* In the physical world, those who listened and filled themselves with irregularities, when they arrive in the hereafter, a darkened holographic projection from themselves surrounds them. Read *Sura 45 Verse 33* what manifests is due to their own rejection of the truth. If you reject love, surrender, trust and truth because of lessons you are going through, you will take that rejection with you on your return to the hereafter. The best way to experience the truth is to feel it through the eyes of love. The activities that take place on the Earth and the interior of Heaven and Hell are according to our states of mind. As you know, states of mind change. Much of what exists only exists because we bring it into existence.

Let us look at the simplicity of the Spiritual Law of Attraction. You attract to yourself according to the thoughts you entertain. You attract because of something that exists within you, something that you have allowed to manifest.

Even in your difficult times, try your best to focus on expressing love. If you find you are struggling, sit in meditation. Do something you enjoy, something that takes your mind off your problems. Meditation is indeed removing yourself away from inner irregularity. As you surrender, what troubled you will become subdued. When you are overwhelmed, self-restraint is the next best thing. Let God see that you know truth from error, that you are strong and firm in your belief. To try is better than not to try at all. Let love manifest itself within you. Disperse the irregular activity that seeks to smother your light.

The light of your inner self is always there guiding you on your pathway. There is no end to the light in the same way there must be an end to irregularity. You can subdue the ego and bring it under the influence of your greater self. When subdued and transformed into light, the ego becomes a great motivator in the bringing about a change. As it walks with you on your pathway, direct it in a way that transforms it into determination.

There is no death for the spirit filled with love and light. Their passing is like stepping outside on a clear sunny day and what a beautiful feeling and sight beholds them. In your daily life and meditations, activate your loving feelings, building love on love, which creates light on light. Your light shines because you have removed yourself from that which darkens you.

Sura 3 Verse 78
78. There is among them a section who distort the book with their tongues.

This is a book. A book can also be a group of thoughts together in one place. You are thought activity in motion. When you speak, you read and interpret the energy that swirls in and around you. You know these as your thought patterns. They are impressions on your mind. According to the images and the intensity they impress on you is according to your action or reaction. What impresses on you from the Heavens can help you see beyond irregularity. The former verse also has references to *Sura 47 Verse 31* in respect to the words; *'and we shall try your reported (mettle)'*. Wisdom fortifies the foundations of your inner self from attack and makes you as strong as iron.

When you think about what thoughts are, you realise you are in-fact always channelling spiritual energy. However, in limited awareness there is a belief that what we express is due to our own cleverness. However, as you open your awareness, you realise it is God who is guiding you. His inspiration is showing you all that you need to know. It is God who creates and clears the way ahead for you. He sends you inspiration as He moves you here and there. He does this so that you might learn what you need to learn. He does this to complete His favours on you.

You can manifest loving feelings, transforming irregularity into light. Let love soothe and comfort these children who refuse to surrender. Can you not see God watching as the two ends of your polarity battle it out? You are the one in the middle deciding who will receive the generated inspiration. In your choice, does the lower-self devour the energy? Alternatively, do you let the evolved self, help you build a ship that will take you through the great seas?

How determined are you to rise and express your full potential? It is not always easy to choose the way that will not ruffle and shake you out of your comfort zone. Awaken the sleeping giant within. Let it do battle against irregular thought activity. You have to fight against all forms of falsehood. Before you go into battle, you have to recognise and identify your true enemy. By the time many people recognise the enemy it has already taken a strong hold.

When misdirected in the use of your emotions, it is easier to overlook the truth that arises. When you are in doubt, check your feelings. Has your consciousness moved to be among your dense crowd of irregularities? You should not turn your back or change the words of truth that come to you. They are your means of right guidance. They are all you have to save you. As you strive, you have to decide for yourself, from which pool do you drink? *Sura 57 Verse 25* talks about iron that comes down from Heaven, not the Earthly iron used to make machinery, tools and other daily items. The things we build from iron come from the elements of the Earth. Reason is a tool that shapes and sharpens our perception. Wisdom helps and guides us on our journey. From it, we extract good things to eat. From it, we build and strengthen ourselves with understanding. In time, you will become mentally as strong as iron. Many people will have heard the statement; 'Such and such a person has a will of iron'. You must learn to wield truth like a sword of justice. However, do not let irregularity make you arrogant. You cannot afford to let negative thoughts dull the tools you use to defeat the onslaught of forces against you. Use wisdom in the way you deal with matters, putting across the truth in a loving, kind, clear manner. You do not need to shout at people. All your good thoughts keep you filled with light. They become the clothes you wear. Steadfastness and determination direct your focus of attention. In the same way you bathe the physical body, you should take time out, submerging your inner self in God's light. Repeat this affirmation to bathe in that light.

In truth there is wisdom
It flows through my soul.
It sits like a letter within my heart.
Closed eyes will reveal its secrets to me.
As I read what is sent in truth, let the dance begin.

There is another saying: 'Get to know the knower behind all that is known.' Ponder on the inspiration behind your loving feelings. You will eventually get to know the spirit guide behind all your thoughts of wisdom. As you exercise your freewill, you weigh up how you feel about the thoughts you entertain. If you do not need what manifests, you discard it and maybe look at it later. The rest, you check for value and sort out into order of merit. As you filter your thoughts, you choose which direction you sail your ship.

Sura 2 Verse 75
75. Seeing that a party of them heard the word of God, and perverted it knowingly after they understood it.

Each person makes for himself or herself a decision. Thoughts of inspiration help us keep the balance. They act as a guide as we enter each of our experiences. Those who strive to live within their loving truth follow more accurately their book, as God planned it.

Sura 26 Verses 224-225
224. And the poets. It is those straying in evil, who follow them:
225. Seest thou not that they wander distracted in every valley?

The Quran is a book that explains the virtues that will help you. It teaches you about a way through the false concepts thrown up by the irregularities. It points the way through your maze of thoughts to the inner garden where all people are invited. On your journey to reach the garden of your inner self, many opportunities will present themselves. Some are but the endings of matters that were not fully resolved the last time you entered the lesson. You must finalise the completion of each lesson. Alternatively, are you entering situations to help end them? To keep you on the best of pathways, previous thoughts that you have constructed rise up to remind you of a past revelation or belief you once held. Meditate and use a bright piercing flame to burn away and transform the old into the new. The old growth must be plucked out from the garden and new seeds nurtured and harvested to bring about change. Work but keep a check on your appetite. The things that are yours will come to you at the right time and place. Live life, enjoying what you do and the rewards of what you do will find their way into your life. Listen to the wisdom from the light, it will suggest to you when you are stepping outside its needs.

Sura 6 Verse 24
24. Behold! How they lie against their own souls! But the (lie) which they invented will leave them in the lurch.

Do not be influenced by those who give flowery discourses and change the truth into something that has a foundation built on irregularity. What is false must disappear, what is true will endure forever. A false interpretation is associating God with something, it is telling a lie against God. Start paying a little bit more attention to what you believe, think or accept as truth. You have feelings to help you do this. Through them, you receive the best guidance. The distinction between truth and error is clear. You hold the balance in your own hands. It is for you to detect the use of words of light built on a foundation of intellectual irregularity. The complainers and haters will never win over the light.

You can become a beautiful spiritual being of light and love, so to believe that you are only your Earthly labels and opinions is putting great limitations on yourself. You are not allowing that part of you that is great to express itself through you. Instead, you live your life as if the godly qualities in the expression of the love you feel do not exist within yourself. You settle for the limited expressions of the emotional conscious self as it plays around in three-dimensional activities.

Realise how beautiful each person really is. If you were to describe yourselves as a musical note, a vibrant pulsating light in the universe. This would be a much more accurate diagnosis than when you think of yourselves only as the physical body and your Earthly conditioning.

Read *Sura 17 Verse 36 and Sura 21 Verse 47* and understand that you can generate thoughts and those thoughts can be a driving force that will expand your inner light. Every thought you have manifest will be enquired into in the hereafter. It is essential that you raise your consciousness. Work with love and you will see the evidence of God's existence with your own eyes. A light will manifest itself before you.

Let us again look at this faculty called, 'the intellect'. It is exactly that. It is no more than a faculty for organising, evaluating and separating the thought process. For some people, it is like a barrier between the light and the darkness. What most people call intelligence is no more than the ability to regenerate thoughts in a certain way. Learning to express yourself in a particular way does not make you cleverer than someone else. Neither is memory recall a sign of intelligence. Do you really want to know what true intelligence is? True intelligence is the ability to love all. Work to save life instead of working to disrupt life. What could be simpler than that? Work for God and the angels of light. Help other people on the journey. We must return there is no doubt and actually, in what condition we return, is what matters. Do you return worn-out and weary from hard work? Alternatively, do you return not realising you have returned? Or, will your return leave you bewildered at the details of the record kept about your life? One way or another, you will return.

Chapter 15: Other Religions; Surrender

With reference to this chapter, read *Sura 3 verse 85; Sura 2 Verse 62;* and *Sura 2 Verses 111-112* and *Sura 22 verse 67.*

The most thought about idea is who is right and who is wrong. No one is actually right and no one is actually wrong. We each organise information in our own minds according to the depth, breadth and width we perceive ourselves to be. Does your vain desire tell you that your beliefs are the only ones that are true? Truly, a vain desire you wish were true. Truly, irregularity divides people, seeking to separate them instead of joining them in unity. Think about any relationship. How long do you think any relationship built on irregularity will last? What you find in irregularity creates separation. Love joins all people in unity. When you hear people say; 'One day Islam (surrender to God) will be the only religion in the world'. Is their interpretation from the tribal self, making their understanding but a vain opinion? Through the evolved self, we will learn a more balanced way of understanding the meaning of the word Islam. For example, 'One day the people who live on the face of the Earth will surrender their wills in love, trust and truth to God, thus Islam is established'. This approach will expand the inner core essence of love, truth and trust within you. The word Muslim means 'someone who surrenders to God'. God wants you to surrender your will to Him. You can do this through following that beautiful small voice within yourself. Do not look at those who follow something different to you with a mind of disbelief. God knows, you do not know. He does not want you to follow men who sit in their ivory towers, built on the sand cliffs. These individuals are propped on their stools by other men. There will always be people of a different religious orientation to you. When you look within yourself, you will see the way forward. Surrendering is about following your inner love, trust and truth, allowing the good and light to manifest as you come up struggling for yourself. Do not be one of those who say only a Muslim will enter paradise without explaining the meaning of the word Muslim. Otherwise, it is vain talk, based on nothing but conjecture. As you put together words for a conversation, your spiritual self, acts as a witness about your own existence as you express yourself.

Do not be of those who doubt and accept another meaning over what they know to be true. Do they speak from their tribal self to your tribal self and as it swells up it creates a place of destitution? Do not be of those who puff out their chests with pride. Surround what manifests and bothers you in the land with love.

The divine expression behind the words in the Holy books is love. As you build light on light, you will find that within each degree there is a feeling of love that gives you an insight and a deeper understanding. Each degree of love brings forth a new insight that creates a new vision. Those who cannot see and therefore do not understand, will put forth their argument about who is and who is not going to Heaven. However, they do not see or know the heart as God knows the heart. While you are living on this Earth, you can transform the foundation of the base matter that surrounds you. You will get enough proof if you seek the home of the hereafter.

Truth and trust are universal and cannot become locked into a particular institution. Work to generate loving thoughts that are in line with your inner voice of love and wisdom. Let your inner journey lead you to those who love you and put you before the material things of this world. All the prophets followed and received inspiration and instructions from the same God, be that directly or via an angel. Do not be afraid to look past those running about on the surface as they mix up their understanding. You will never know freedom until you have freed your mind of the irregularities that limit you. Those men and women, who have the spiritual strength, reach out, tapping into the rivers of energy and extract the truth they find there. Search for the truth wherever you can find it. If you are in doubt, meditate, the answers will arrive. For further reading, you can read *Sura 22 verse 67*. If you belong to a group, it does not mean all other people have to adopt those ceremonial or ritualistic ways of approach to God.

Examine your thoughts, throwing out the things that have outgrown their usefulness. Do not be afraid to seek the truth. One religious sect and its peoples do not have the sole rights to the love, truth, trust and wisdom of God. People are tapping into the spiritual nature of themselves. We are slowly beginning to awaken to the awareness of the workings of the Spiritual Laws. As we do, we can send out from ourselves what will be of benefit to humanity. The Spiritual Laws are like a mirror and reflect back to us the things we manifest or have manifest. The love we send out will come back to us, as love multiplied by love. Teach your children how they can use their feelings to guide themselves through life. They will live their lives the way you teach them. Teach them to live in love.

Teaching your children to meditate will enable them to focus and gain stability in their expression. The inner beauty that they create will sustain them. They will gain a greater amount of inner strength to deal with their life's experiences. Give them a foundation of positive thoughts that will keep them energised and spiritually alert. Combine this with an excellent philosophy; then, both yours and their lives will flourish.

There is no difference between you and the people you call prophets. The exception is that they are the essence of the love, trust and truth that comes to you. These men and women raised their consciousness up to the Heavens. They are a greater expression of the godly qualities that exist within you. Understand this, we are each only aware according to our own spiritual state of consciousness.

God presents Himself to us as light. Abraham recognised the truth and surrendered his will. As you surrender to God, you will find Heaven. Even if you do not belong or associate yourself to a particular group, through the act of love, you stand at the door to the kingdom of God.

Sura 21 Verse 30
30. We made from water every living thing. Will they not then believe?

Ice is water in its coldest form. As it heats up and melts, it changes its form. When it begins to boil, it changes to steam and then disappears as it evaporates from sight. Yet, it continues to be there as moisture in the air.

The inner self's vibrations are similar to a wavelength frequency. It is like the sound of a note made by a musical instrument; the lower the note the slower its vibration, the higher the note the quicker its vibration. This physical world and its content is spiritual energy vibrating at a slow rate. However, the inner self vibrates at a rate beyond the vision perceived by our physical eyes. It vibrates according to the degree of its spiritual expression of love. Irregular thinking creates dark spots in the inner self, slowing down its vibration. Expressing loving feelings fills you with light, speeding up your inner self's vibrations. The effect of love on your inner self is like switching on a light.

Your thoughts influence the vibrational frequencies of your inner self. The place you call the afterlife is varying degrees of vibrational frequencies. In the physical world, two people who are spiritually at different ends of the Spiritual Law of Polarity can occupy the same place. In the hereafter, spirits separate through the Law of Attraction, each going to a place that vibrates according to their inner self's expression. Repeat this affirmation to speed up your vibration.

I fill my soul with light to see.
Beyond the solid forms.
Oh, soul vibrate at a faster rate

That I may change to a higher state.

What makes particles solid is their vibration and composition of energy. Objects vibrating at the same or similar frequency can appear as solid forms to each other. To disperse or make disappear any solid forms, you can raise its energy vibration. A focus of concentrated energy can alter the molecular structure of physical matter. First, learn to feel and work with the different compositions of energy, sound and light. As you do it will heal, balance and restore. The energy you generate can stabilise or destabilise matter. Filling yourself with love, builds up your inner light. This raises your spirit's vibration. Vibrating on a higher frequency, you ascend through the degrees of consciousness. Eventually you reach the greater states of awareness. Thus, you are able to see and speak with those who dwell there. Illness in the body is the destabilisation that takes place in matter. Healing is the stabilisation of matter. In the physical reality, nothing is solid because spirit can pass through what appears to be dense structures. All life is a creation of light particles, which are vibrating at different rates, giving them their density. One of the best ways to heal and restore something is to express love towards the object of your affection. Darkness does not restore anything. When you have a moment to yourself, send out loving thoughts to all people in the same disposition as you or the same physical condition as you may have. As the energy, which you send out must first pass through you, let the healing begin.

In the hereafter, spirits vibrating at the same rate are solid forms to each other. If one spirit raises its vibration and the other lowers its vibration, the lower one may lose their awareness of the higher one. However, the one residing in the greater state would not necessary lose awareness of the lower one. How do those beings in the hereafter come to us on Earth? They lower and slow down their vibrational frequency making themselves detectable or visible to those they come to see. They bring a message of love and hope. In the same way, they lower their vibrations as they come to you, you have to raise your conscious awareness to a vibration, which you can spiritually see, hear and communicate with them. To do this, you must leave the land where you dwell. Your inner manifestation must be one of loving surrender. Express love and you will fill with light and it will make the contact more desirable.

Energy and inspiration come to you like clouds. With closed eyes, you will see how beautiful their patterns are as they appear before you. These shapes eventually clump together to create one light. As the light enshrouds you, you will feel its energy washing through, over and around you. From the clouds, you extract a message that is right for you. Sometimes you discard the best thoughts you have in a pretence you do not hear or understand them. However, inspiration never gives up lighting the way through the turmoil to bring you a message. Work to improve your ability to hold on to the best of what you hear. Do not let wisdom slip away to become buried beneath falsehoods.

Sura 83 Verse 23
23. On thrones (of dignity) will they command a sight (of all things).

Your feelings and thoughts show you your breadth, depth and width. Thoughts are energy. Energy forms like clouds. Energy follows thought, meeting at a destination of the viewer's choice.

As you raise your consciousness, your vision opens and sees what is usually behind a veil. You begin to command a sight of all things. When *The Quran* refers to; *'those who can see'*, it is talking about those who can see clearly using their spiritual vision. What flows through the inner self shows up on the screen of your mind. The modern-day terminology for; *'commanding a sight of all things'*, is *'remote viewing'*. All things vibrate and with vibrations, there must be sound. All energy is interconnected. You can direct your attention and spiritually enquire into what you focus on. With practice, you will know how to feel and read the vibrations of any object, extracting information from its written record. With spirit, time and space as they are perceived on Earth does not exist, there is simply being. All the things within the inner self's polarity become accessible to those who practice *muraqabah*. Now that you are paying attention; 'And you thought those who meditate were only sitting there with their eyes closed thinking la-di-dah thoughts'. People who meditate and expand their consciousness know there is a big difference between being still and doing nothing.

What you call imagination is a glimpse into the creative self through the mind. What you call the mind is like a door to your inner self. The body does not have an imagination; it is a vehicle so that spirit can learn to express itself in love. When you are using what you call imagination, you are really accessing the inner depths of yourself. Your job is to learn to self-manage yourself as the laws impress on you according to your book of deeds.

Sura 34 Verse 52
52. And they will say, "We do believe (now in the truth)"; but how could they receive (faith) from a position (so) far off,

The irregularities are all for making this physical world its home. The wisdom of the evolved self is all for making you aware of your spiritual connection to the afterlife. The evolved self wants to make sure your Heavenly home is as comfortable as it can be and so the struggle between the two begins. When you are in the tribal self, you are in a position far from the truth. In a state of bewilderment, many people take what arises from the darkness for their god and with haste follow it. As you learn to change the vibrations of your inner self, knowledge about events to come will guide you. The more you can extract before you return to your dense surroundings, the greater will be your insight.

Sura 76 Verse 3
3. We showed him the way: Whether he be grateful or ungrateful (rests on his will).

Also read, *Sura 34 Verse 46.* As your clairvoyant vision opens, you begin to see what is to come. Each of us receives tests on what it is we follow in life. It is in this that you get to know the depth, breadth and width of your own inner self. As you move around in your home, attaching yourself to the things created out of the Earth, try not to lose sight of what is important.

Be aware of your feelings of contentment, they will let you know on which foundation you have built your house. Become aware of the winds that swirl around your vessel. When you see what you thought you once possessed slipping away from your grasp, try not to follow it to the ends of the Earth. Let what you borrowed, go with the same kind of joy you felt as it entered your life.

God does not change, His words do not change, the pathway does not change, His light does not change and His love does not change. What changes are the degrees you can see, hear and learn to live your life. Has that little voice of wisdom ever not been there for you? Help will always be there. What is ordained to reach you, will reach you. Surrender yourself to the good thoughts you have. If you ignore the thoughts of right actions and good behaviour, you are not surrendering yourself to divine guidance. All that you receive will be recorded and your account will show if you listened or not. Refer to *Sura 3 Verse 118 and Sura 3 Verse 71.*

Sura 74 Verse 4
4. And thy garments keep free from stain!

Look at some of the situations that surround you. How many of them are real? How much is your own logical and emotional-self's imagined activity? If you had allowed the inspiration from the Heavens to flourish in your life, your perception of the situations around you would appear different. The wisdom you receive prepares you for the future events in your life. Your thoughts create the garments of your inner self. They are the clothes you will appear in when called to account. Keep your inner self free from the stains of irregularity. The best clothes are full of love and radiate with light.

One thought of truth can extinguish many thoughts of untruth. But untruth will never extinguish truth. It does not matter how many falsehoods you pile on top. The truth is truth; falsehood is falsehood. You will make a full circle and come back to the truth you covered up. Let your experiences strengthen you, teaching you to stand on your own two feet. When you are in the middle of your inner war, strive to defeat the enemy with love.

As for those who think their lineage or name gives them a spiritual position or rank above another, they are mistaken. This concept of lineage does not give anyone an automatic entrance to Heaven. This is no more than a figment of their imaginations, a constructed idea from lower desires in a bid to gain your approval. It is but a show as they dwell among their vain desires. Each one of us will always reap what we have sown as we come up struggling for ourselves.

Everyone you have ever met or visually seen is predestined into your life. Some people will stay around you while other people go their way according to God's laws. You know the person who keeps entering your life and you wish they would pack up their bags and depart. They will not leave until you have spiritually satisfied certain conditions. These obligations are not necessary towards them but towards yourself. If something irritates you, look within yourself. Being hostile towards the irritation will not bring about an end to it. Whatever is irritating you may leave for a while. However, it will be back one day because you did not learn your lesson fully according to the law. Only through love will you learn to heal your irritation.

To recap a little from Chapter 10, Adam and Eve: A part of your spiritual group can have a life in another society and culture gaining experiences they will take back to the group. When you wage war and shout hatred at other people, it is like waging war against yourself. The people you encounter, that pass right by you, even those who you see across the street have a spiritual connection to you in some way. The people you meet or shout at can be members of your own spiritual family group. They are coming into your life or vision to teach you lessons of love, friendship and compassion. Spiritual families extend far beyond any Earthly ideas about families, cultures and traditions. Your rank is your spiritual state and has nothing to do with where you think you came from, your class or caste or who you think you are. Your name in the hereafter can be different from the name that you have in this world.

Be prepared to recognise that within you is everything you need to succeed. Within the lands beyond this world, you will find all the love and encouragement you need. The easiest way to control an individual is to keep them ignorant and allow fear and insecurities to undermine their spiritual ability to grow. Negative emotion builds an unstable foundation, which leaves you open to false desires. Do you end up running around trying to build a stable foundation based on the things that are external to yourself? You will find each pathway presented to you as an option contains varying degrees of dualistic activity. You will receive your answers through wisdom and it will calm down the irregularity. In that moment of surrender, you are able to break down challenging tasks into smaller manageable parts.

Chapter 16: Flirt with the Ego

Sura 3 Verse 30
30. "On the day when every soul will be confronted with all the good it has done, it will wish there were a great distance between it and its evil."

To flirt with the ego is like dancing with the Devil. The ego has a way of driving you on a pathway that leads to nowhere. It does not care whom or what gets in its way as it expresses itself. When there is scheming in the mind, evil will add to it, manipulating whatever situation it can, even truth itself, to get what it wants. As you flirt between your polarity around which you cycle, you will come to realise this is but a game, it can be a very dangerous game.

Do not engage yourself with this dance or let it tempt and draw you out from the light. Be aware of the vision that you hold about the one you call the evil one and do not associate it to something and somewhere it is not. As you reflect on your reaction and your action to the things that take place before you, ask yourself; 'Is my perception a reflection of the light or do I feed the ego and dance with the Devil?'

Be aware which direction your intention comes and goes. In its wake will be either love or war. With intention, follows thought and with thought follows the energy as you walk the path that you have chosen for yourself.

Read *Sura 14 Verse 22* and understand that as you immerse yourself in the world, if you are not careful, you will find yourself dicing with death itself. There are those unfortunate people who wage war against God and themselves. People who flirt with the ego can only lose because it drives them deeper and deeper into the depths of bewilderment and despair. Truly, desperation engulfs them and they dim the light of their own inner sanctuary.

Satan said; 'He promises you, however, then he fails to keep it'. The force behind your irregularities has no power of its own. It uses your own will against you. Is your ability to see open, but the leaning in your mind is towards the world of irregularity? Are the thoughts that show up on the screen of your mind corrupted? Are you fooled into believing what comes to you comes from God? When what you see does not manifest, confusion and doubt surface. You then turn your focus of attention to God believing that He is the one who has let you down. However, you fail to understand that you heard but did not see from where your information came. It is for you to reproach your own inner self through reason as to why you think your best-laid plans did not manifest.

You are a co-creator of your destiny and you will find that error, when given the chance, will work through you using your own willpower to manifest and create. When the error does manifest, you will see and hear the manifesters complain.

As you reduce the flirting in the land, there will appear a light in the highest horizon. From a faint star, this light evolves into a bright sun. As the land becomes fertile, it starts to flourish. The flowers in the garden will not release their exotic fragrance until you have created the right conditions. As you walk among the new growth, your presence will have an effect on the garden. As the gentle winds blow and you follow your path, the flowers in the garden surrender fragrances that sweeten your world.

Sura 33 Verse 29
29. But if ye seek God and His apostle, and the home of the hereafter, verily God has prepared for the well-doers amongst you a great reward.

The hereafter is not in some far distant place that is unreachable; situated in a distant location, galaxy, or unknown part of the universe. It is accessible right here, right now. The journey is not too difficult, it is a matter of paying attention to your thoughts and feelings. It is a matter of listening and allowing yourself to attune too and feel God's loving subtle energies, using your own energy. Expressing the godly qualities within love is the surest way of attracting the attention of those beings in the hereafter. The loving energies sent from God contain all that you need to know about the journey home. They are working with you, helping you to subdue the ego. As you continue to listen, you will realise that your feelings of love will carry you all the way to Heaven.

To know something of God seek His face, seek His light within. You see it within the mind. If you filled your mind with clutter, you will not see the light. Push on through, past what makes you swerve. Through your mind, you will enter the place where you will find God's face smiling at you. His face is in a place of peace and solitude. In this place, learn how to work with His Spiritual Laws and channel His energy in a loving way. The distinction is clear between the ends of your polarity. If you continue to flirt with the ego, you will forever struggle to enter and hold yourself within the light.

Surrendering to your feelings of love will elevate your consciousness. On your life's journey, you will experience both beauty and turbulence as the road before you is broken down and then rebuilt, and then broken down and rebuilt with love. Each time the road is built, your journey becomes a little shorter, a little straighter. The road gets straighter in that you remain longer within the light and shorter in that you get closer to God.

Like a stream flowing, some flow gentler. The trickle of a small stream or brook as it winds its way down the hillside can be more beautiful than the rush of a large turbulent river.

You have spiritually agreed beforehand to all that takes place in your life. It is for you to seek, listen, learn and create a foundation of wisdom to help you understand your experiences. The greater your love, the more understanding and radiant your inner light becomes. Through the light, you will know what the wise ones know as you walk along the road less travelled.

At some point, you created a thought consciously or unconsciously, that activated the experiences you have been through and will undergo as part of your learning and development.

Chapter 17: *Jihad*

Jihad means different things to different people. For some people, the word brings to the surface the darkest realities of their inner self. Do they not understand how and when to implement its meaning for the greater good of all? As you climb through the degrees of light and awareness, you will become more enlightened about where the real struggle should be taking place. In our struggles, as our consciousness points in the direction of the physical world, our trials and tests give us a chance to see how we are progressing. We become aware of what we need to do to improve ourselves. However, there is also another striving that is important. It is the struggle within oneself to overcome our attachments and irregularities. There is striving for God or struggling to cope with the inner vision, we create about our external reality.

The word *Jihad* means 'to strive'. However, as time went by other meanings have also become associated to it. For clarity about this, read *Sura 17 verse 73*. You can also read *Sura 2 verse 75* and *Sura 3 verse 78*. Do not substitute a lesser meaning over the revelation of a higher meaning. The way many people interpret *Jihad* today is from the word Holy War used by the crusaders of old Christianity. A quick reminder, majority thinking does not make it right. Is the majority thinking astray from the path? Is irregularity trying to replace the true meaning? There is one place you can truly implement the meaning associated to the word *Jihad* and know you are implementing it in the best of ways. It is in your own struggle against your own lower desires and irregularities as you seek the face of God. Refer to *Sura 2 Verse 272*.

Sura 6 Verse 116
116. Wert thou to follow the common run of those on Earth. This verse then goes on to say; *They follow nothing but conjecture: they do nothing but lie.*

The Prophet Muhammad is a prophet of love. Before he started his mission, he secluded himself away in the cave of Hira and meditated.

You will find sect may rise against sect; group against group; neighbour against neighbour. God will plan what He plans. It is not for you to cast judgement as to how God decides to manifest and pluck people from the world. Do you want to see a change to God's ways on Earth? Then you must change; refer to *Sura 13 Verse 11*. Those who do good will be in their right places helping the lost ones. When you look to the spiritual, you will find the winner of the battle. Can you name a battle in the material world that has led to peace among its people? Many people can tell you the results of the battle they had to cleanse their inner self. In the end, they found Heaven and God's word to be true. God sees into the hearts of all people, guiding all to the place of their departure, so ready yourself for that inevitable day.

All life is but different densities of spiritual light. According to how you perceive that light, will determine the way you choose to work and strive in the name of God. There are those who try to manipulate what they see, pushing and shoving things around until they believe they fit into their conditioned programme of beliefs, laws, expressions and perceptions. The best workers use love and compassion as they work with the external environment. To put the best construction on the word *Jihad* it is to recognise the battle within oneself. Is it not best to first put your own house in order? As you raise your consciousness, you will see things in a clearer light. Love will fill you with compassion. As you consciously ascend, striving to raise yourself up in the direction of the greater conscious states, duality disappears leaving you with one love, one trust and one truth. Irregular energy is a life force. It does not want to dissolve back into the oneness, into the light. When its existence is threatened, it fights back.

Sura 22 Verse 15

*15. Let him stretch out a rope to the ceiling and cut (himself) off:
then let him see whether his plan will remove what enrages (him)!*

Again, read *Sura 45 Verse 33* and consider what happens to those
who reject the truth and become enraged, are they but a product of
skilful manipulation? They refuse to turn their back and instead
rush head long into what they know can destroy them. Their anger
will avail them nothing. Neither will those who are, through skilful
manipulation, enraged and become martyrs. As their chosen
pathway manifest before them, they catapult themselves into their
deepest darkest depths. When they arrive in the hereafter, they
carry with them the irregular beliefs they held. The expression on
which they built their life encircles them. Are you sure, you are
fighting for truth and not any other reason? Are you sure, your
spiritual self is in the best possible state it could have achieved
while on the planet Earth? You yourself are the house of God; bricks
and mortar are but bricks and mortar. As you move through life,
respect the vehicle that you use to travel through the land. Most of
all respect the vehicles you use as you travel the inner journey. The
movements, flows and migrations of life are the movements and
flows of energy as it interacts and balances itself out. How and why
it moves, flows and intermingles in a particular way is not for you to
complain and protest about. You should take great care about the
direction you lean in the mind as you travel; for what is within you
becomes stronger the more you feed it.

If you deliberately and meaningfully commit suicide because of
something you think is happening to you, it is a crime against
yourself and the whole of humanity. If you decide to end your life,
you have not transcended the irregularities, you have become
consumed by them. Such a sad and difficult time for those left
behind. The one who ends up in the hereafter, after suffering such a
distressful matter is cared for with love. There act is not viewed in
the same way by those in the hereafter as those who
indiscriminately murder others. You know that God does not get
things wrong. Try not to create irregular thoughts about the

movement of matter and its comings and goings to and from this world. God's love will indeed surround and heal you, restoring you, teaching you in truth.

What portion of the foundation of yourself came from those around you? Did you accept without question what other people told you and lost your way? Did you read but did not listen to the wisdom of your evolved self? Your life unfolds according to your book of deeds. Your attachments to the events in your life are in your control. Question everything and do not accept what you feel is wrong. The thoughts that rise from the manipulation of the truth suggest to you that in some way God got things wrong. His wisdom has always been guiding you. What you are going through is not because God got it wrong. Did you accept something built on a foundation of love or irregularity? The physical world is not an illusion that needs to be changed. It is real. Two people looking at the same situation will each have their own ideas about what is taking place. The thoughts that arise regarding what you are looking at shapes your perception. The real illusions are the irregular thoughts you entertain. However, God is full of compassion and enquires into everything with love.

Sura 24 Verse 39
39. But the unbelievers, their deeds are like a mirage in sandy deserts, which the man parched with thirst mistakes for water.

You will come to know the poetry of the unbelievers from the words they speak. You go to them thinking they may quench your thirst. Do not be disillusioned, God will quench your thirst. God is ever with you. Ride the wave of despair, turning inwards for your answers. God knows what is happening within the depths of your spiritual self. God has given you freewill, allowing you to choose between the light and the darkness. The love and light within you will not allow you to go astray.

There are those who reach the limit of their awareness at an early age and so turn to the world to complete what they believe is an understanding towards their growth. On top of their light and love, they store the conclusions about their Earthly experiences. It will be many years before they look below this foundation they have built on top of the light. Their cup fills to the top and overflows with the ways of the world. When you build up your foundation on soft sands, it will not last. Be prepared to embrace change. Those of you who do not cover up their love, continually drink from the heart of God. As you drink from the everlasting cup, your awareness has room to grow in every direction. Each one of us is able to turn around and lean towards God's love and drink. Love is a constant expression of God. Each one of us has within, a light. This ensures there is always a direction you can turn, always the potential for you to grow and find your way home.

Refer to *Sura 22 Verse 25* and Sura 59 Verse 14 and know that there will always be room for the expression of love to manifest itself through you. Do not be a complainer. Do not be like those who push and shove. The tribal self's main concern is for its own self. In its opposition to God, it does not care about anything and will attack whatever gets in the way of what it desires for itself. Let those who act tough and enjoy fighting, fight the irregularities within their own self. Truly, this battle will bring the true champion to the surface. In your surrender and withdrawal from your irregularities, you will learn amazing things about yourself. When the verse says; *'equal is the dweller there'*, it is making you aware of the Spiritual Law of Attraction. You attract to yourself, or you are attracted to, according to what you send out in thought. In the hereafter, you end up in a place according to your inner state of being.

When a Muslim complains and acts out of rage against other religious groups that God has established in the land, they are not thinking about what *The Quran* is actually saying. The former verse is clear; it says; *'As a result, it fills the unbeliever with rage at them.'*

The true believers do not cause indiscriminate death. Read the very first Sura in *The Quran*. *Verse 7* says; *'those whose portion is not wrath.'* Your inner love must override what arises as irregularity. The true believer is compassionate and caring for all people, no matter which faith they follow. The faith God has established for other people is according to His will. It is God who has established the teaching within *The Taurat* (*The Torah*, the Jewish Holy book) and the true Christian Gospels. To complain or be enraged because they are not following what you believe, makes you an unbeliever. If you dislike something, surrender to God. If you believe they are wrong, God will judge them, not you. The verses in *The Quran* explain this but you choose to ignore this wisdom and truth. The rage you hold on to will surround you in the afterlife. What comes from the mouths of those who complain or those who become filled with rage does so through their choice? They have chosen not to surrender. They have opened the door to their negative emotions and their beasts charge forth like a stampede.

God's way is to do all things through love. As your spiritual vision opens, God shows Himself to you as the inner light you see. As God becomes the dweller within your sacred mosque, His throne of authority establishes itself within you. As it does, you ascend up to the Heavens. God's workers will use the love and light that flows from God. They use their knowledge of the Spiritual Laws to carry out their work for God. Their challenge is to ensure that they hold their consciousness steady in the light. Recognise the body as an instrument, which you use for expanding your conscious awareness. In your research, you learn to co-operate, working in unity with the greater order. Join other people in this work to bring in the new changes. Use your godly qualities to kindle the light of your inner self. Fill yourself with this light and send the light out into the world during your meditations.

The practice of *muraqabah* keeps you from becoming an inactive doubter who refuses to surrender. Meditation gives you an opportunity to become an active participant in the fight against irregularities. You become a part of the family who seek to work as a single unit of light. Within each religious group, there are those who feel this stirring in themselves. Listen and hear the call from the light. Feel the need to visit the sacred place within. The true seekers of God must learn to direct their feelings appropriately. God has created a light by which He guides you. You need to recognise God's love through the expression of your feelings, learning to direct yourself in a way that reduces the pull of the irregularities. You cannot deny the truth; you can overcome falsehood.

As we explore some more, read *Sura 9 Verse 107* and think about what is the mosque the *infidels* (people who do not believe in God) erect? It is their own self, driven on by the tribe and their own will and the desires of their irregularities. Those who dwell within their tribal self are forever trying to disunite the believers, tempting them down from their solitude. Remember, Islam is a state of mind and not a state-of-the-art building. Through the practice of *muraqabah,* you can maintain and kindle the sacred flame of the inner sacred mosque. As you express love, the doorways to the gardens of Heaven open. You will eventually stand with those beings who reside in the house of God, having reached the spiritual station of light.

Refer to *Sura 93 Verses 6-9*. An orphan is usually associated with a child whose parents have passed away or abandoned them so they are not physically involved in their upbringing. Another kind of orphan is one surrounded by those who are spiritually dead while they are alive. The child sees and knows things hidden from the blinded people. When the child tries to get answers, few people can give them explanations. The spiritual orphan tries to fit in with what is going on, yet remain puzzled by the delights that other people indulge in. In falsehood, they are lost, unable to function properly in the same way they would function if surrounded by people of understanding. Words of harshness about their enquiry puzzle them deeply. Therefore, they retreat until they meet those who can teach them to open the inner way.

People who recognise what will draw them up, work in stillness, silence and love. They will pass right by you and you would not know them. They have been through what you now go through and have transcended it. They have worked hard, dedicated themselves, practiced until their fruits are ripe. They learn true respect for the loving energy they work with. It is now time for you to live in the light, meet new friends and discover new worlds. All the while, you were under the protection of God. You had to learn and understand the ways of the doubters. You must remain independent of those around you who are dependent on each other for support. Whereas they are unsure, you are free to explore, seeing beyond the complaints they make about how the Spiritual Laws are governing their journey. Instead, join up with those who are a witness to the truth and the trust. The centre of the sacred mosque is not out of your reach. For people who strive, the doors will open and they will enter.

Refer to *Sura 5 Verse 65 and Sura 9 Verse 108.* There are many people so accustomed and comfortable with what comes from the tribal self; when thoughts arise from their feelings of truth, they are like a foreign language to them. As they reflect in the mind, the tribe lurking in the shadows attacks the wisdom of their evolved self. The truth is not beaten, it retreats for a while, waiting, watching, like the little worm that gnawed away at the stick of Solomon. Read *Sura 34 Verse 14.* What happens when the truth comes? They use stubbornness to do evil instead of using it for good. They use the favours bestowed on them and challenge the giver of those favours.

Sura 53 Verse 7
7. While he was in the highest part of the horizon:

Refer to *Sura 23 Verse 50.* People who strive to be honest in thought, word and deed have learnt from times gone by, paying caution to the warnings that rise-up within. They are the people who build up their mosques and reside in dwellings on high. They wait and watch as the mosques built on the sand-cliffs crumble to pieces, rebuild themselves and again crumble. They will repeat this as they learn what makes a strong foundation.

Learning is part of life and you will make mistakes. Our lessons do not always fit into our concept of logic yet they can still be in truth. This is because the Spiritual Laws and not customary manmade ways of life govern our lessons. To sail your ship smoothly, you must pay attention. Practice self-restraint when in doubt.

Isa, (Jesus) and his mother Maryam, (Mary) were both of the righteous and given shelter on the high ground. Muhammad also resided within the open spaces of the higher ground. Many people who have walked the face of the Earth have reached the higher ground. You too must learn to reside in the highest part of your horizon. People who reside within mosques on high, descend with truth and wisdom to inspire other people to make the journey. Read *Sura 41 Verse 30.*

Sura 47 Verse 19
19. For God knows how ye move about and how ye dwell in your homes.

The mosque built from the first day on piety exists within each of us. You can enter your inner mosque any time you wish by withdrawing yourself. Read *Sura 9 Verse 109.*

You know you are not the physical body. You have other bodies invisible to the physical eyes but seen by the mind's eye. Neither is the physical reality your real home. Your temporary home is among the worldly thoughts you entertain. Your Heavenly home radiates with the godly qualities of love. Treat yourself the way you treat your material home. From time to time, you should redecorate it, give yourself a new coat of paint, and hang up some new pictures. A home not looked after will eventually crumble. The roof will start to leak; mould will appear on the walls; rot will set in. The framework will start to creak, crack and bend. Decay sets in and the house starts to fall down. The owner of the house then leaves.

Are you strong and able to stand for truth? Build your mosque on the higher ground and it will last forever, sustained by the love and will of God. The battle between the two forces will not cease until what is dark and murky is light and bright. During the transformations that you go through, you may end up in tears because of your perception of the experience. Through the light of your inner self, you perceive a greater understanding and possibility about yourself. Among your tears, you will see the truth as to why the experience was necessary. It is time for you to surrender yourself in love. When you read *The Quran* or any other Holy book brought forth by enlightened individuals, see the wisdom. As you read, you will generate thoughts on which you can build your new home. What you did not see in the first reading will jump out at you during the second. It is not that you missed what was there the first time. What you learnt in the first sitting laid the foundation for the second. Refer to *Sura 90 Verses 10-13*.

Sura 91 Verses 7-10
7. By the soul, and the proportion and order given to it;

Practise this affirmation to help you on your journey.

Bring my life into line
With the light of the Divine.
By the light of my soul
Down that road, I will stroll.

To raise your consciousness, you must travel the road that is steep. *Sura 34 Verses 52-53* explain how those in doubt cast slanders about the hereafter from a position far off. The proportion and order given to you is in accordance with your spiritual needs. You live your life between your light and your darkness, acting according to the portion you accepted. As you travel, the Spiritual Laws impress on you the will of God. As the lesson draws to an end, the conditions that the laws have impressed on you start to dissolve around you. During the experience, as you reflect in the mind, you know within yourself, which way you tilt the scales.

Most people who have the good things of this life do not want a change in the laws that surround them unless they bring in more. However, life is about change. If by having many things of the world, you have to learn a lesson, you will get exactly what you need. When it is time for those things to be withdrawn, a change in circumstances will take place. It is not for anyone to question why some people have and some people have not. Life is ever in motion and does not stop at a particular place to keep you happy. There are points along the path that manifest challenges. If you refuse to express love between these points of change, it will not stop the change in circumstance reaching you. Try your best between the points of your varying fortunes, accepting with love the way the winds blow. Refer to *Sura 34 Verse 37.*

Sura 30 Verse 27
27. To Him belongs the loftiest similitude (we can think of) in the Heavens and the Earth: For He is exalted in might, full of wisdom.

How do you travel to the places on high? You listen to the best of your thoughts. As you follow the advice, you flow with a favourable wind. This is God's way of leading us out of the darkness into the light.

You need to be aware of the difference between true visualisation, dreaming and fantasising. Strive to visualise for the benefit of all people. No harm to any individual becomes a part of that vision or dream. Fantasising is usually for self-gratification. It is the delusion of grandeur. These delusions arise from the beasts that roam through the land. Through the tribal self, many people are continuing to generate and manifest the will of the darkness. It is for you to turn to God and do His will. Try a little harder to rise above your delusions of grandeur. To do God's will, listen to your evolved self. You cannot keep blaming the evil one. After all, you made a choice.

When you live in the highest horizon of your inner self, you will get a glimpse of the path ahead of you. When you arrive at the door of the manifest event, be aware of it. The event will take place. When it arrives, enter, ready to play your part. Because you are aware of this moment, ensure you bring with you an extra amount of love and create a greater outcome. This will set the stage for the next part of your journey. Refer to *Sura 5 Verse 57*. Use this affirmation to reach the bliss of peace within.

Let the light within my soul
Restore a balance in my life.
From war to peace, within myself
Let the calm replace my tears.

Sura 6 Verse 89
89. We shall entrust their charge to a new people who reject them not.

When a matter reaches you, do you surrender to God's divine will or do you fight against it, clinging to the everyday life of the world? When you complain, you are showing that you have not accepted the manifest conditions of what you have agreed? Happy will the believers be as they establish the truth. The customs and traditions the doubters bring with them saying; 'This is from God', will not fool or blind those who reside on high. As God removes the truth from you, He will establish it in the hearts of others who will not reject it.

Sura 61 Verse 8
8. Their intention is to extinguish God's light (by blowing) with their mouths but God will complete (the revelation of) His light, even though the unbelievers may detest (it).

You can never extinguish the light in someone else's heart, nor can you extinguish it in your own. The best you can do is cover the truth for a while. Strive hard on the inner pathway and do not let irregularities cause your vision to swerve. You throw the word *Kafr* (hide or cover truth) around aiming it away from the place it needs to be at rest. Do not be one of those who blame other people but accept responsibility for your own spiritual condition. The road is straight, falsehood makes it a winding one. If the journey were impossible, there would be no point to life but many have gone on before you. Every good deed you leave behind today will one day help you in the future. When you catch up with the deeds you set in motion, you have an opportunity to add to them, making the way ahead easier. As with all things, there are polarities within polarities in the growth of your inner nature. Once you have reached beyond the moon's ocean of emotion, you will marvel at the view. The moon truly has schooled you. Express love as the laws unfold around you. Your spiritual self directs you to your experiences. As you play your part, you educate yourself in the best of ways. Strive to maintain an inner balance. You give life to or can withdraw life from, any of the scenarios within your world.

Listen to the loving melody expressed within. Strive to be the best you can be. Do not let the love, trust and truth within your heart become a foreign language to you. Let it be the only language.

Strive to maintain and hold yourself in the light. When you surrender yourself to the darkness, your expression reflects that state of consciousness. When you surrender yourself to the light, your expression fills with love. In this state, your consciousness ascends to reside in the Heavens.

Chapter 18: Your Inner Truth

Refer to *Sura 35 Verse 32* and *Sura 5 Verse* 88 with reference to this chapter.

Each garden and river above you contains inspiration about the pathway that raises you up into its surroundings. The gardens and rivers that flow underneath you are places you have transcended. You know the lands you have transcended because you turn your back on the beasts that dwell there. You raised your spiritual self to its present station because you saw and discarded that which was of no more use. It is now time for you to move on again. To reach the gardens above you, you have to withdraw your consciousness from the land where you dwell. Your determination holds you steady. The love you manifest expands and carries you into the light of this new land. This land becomes your place of rest where you can quench your thirst in readiness for the next stage of your journey.

People who live in the past will die in the past. What you create about the past maybe so far removed from its real reality, you end up living in nothing more than a fabricated reality. You are not responsible for what anyone else does; you are only responsible for what you think, do, are doing and will do. You have to live for the day, live for the moment. Your inner self does not know the meaning of past, present or future. Your conscious self creates a perception of reality based on what you accept. This is why you must choose with love. Why waste time creating an unreal world to live in?

You will find history divides into three pathways. There are those who make the history. There are those who follow the history and there are people who are the history. What the history makers create is lived by other people. They experience it and then the matter becomes a part of their life's history. History is but the remembrance of an event after the experience. Let inspirational ideas be your guide. All that is with you will outgrow its usefulness. All things will become unnecessary at some point in your life. Do not rely on history but seek the inner truth. You do not have to live by what you created or previously believed in for the rest of your life. Be here in the present and you will learn and understand how to become a history maker.

If you do not open the door to loving surrender but instead, relive through memory recall, the same self-created visions and thoughts, how will you ever know what is beyond where you are? You can become stuck in a cycle of thought activity, which becomes lived by you repeatedly. As you dwell on the memories you hold, how true is what you imagine? Have you invented additional information and added it to the event? All things are in motions and those things held as a memory become unreliable the older they get. Your thoughts and their intensity will create for you a reality. If you follow the ways that you found your fathers following, were they on right guidance or were they astray? The old becomes the new as what we learn is passed from adult to child. We forget the power of thought activity and our ability to add to, imagine and create. It is through such creations our imagined historical conjecture creates a false image about the events and the personalities connected to the events. How can history be so reliable, when in the physical world it is so easy to change or forget some part of it? You may find you apply too much emotional expression to some part of it, thus changing the emphasis and degree in the expression of the facts. With the smallest change of expression comes a new meaning to the event. However, have you accepted these fabricated historical imagined events as true? Is it that you have not learnt to see beyond where you are and so instead, you look backwards? Live in the here, live in the now and strive to accept truth over falsehood. People who make the history are ever in motion, ever reaching out with their consciousness, ever expanding their inner essence and understanding for the benefit of humanity. Eventually, other people explore what they create, using it as a stepping-stone, never to return to the old ways.

You can change what is within you through love. You will not find a change in God's ways. However, you will find a change in what man says. All that you manifest through love benefits humanity. Do not let yourself be lost in the past. When you focus on your development, you stop reflecting on the past.

In the beginning, God created the light and the darkness. It is through our desires that the interior of the light and the darkness becomes what it is. Through expressing love, your godly qualities grow and expand. You can generate a great amount of light. A hypothetical example is that of a light bulb. Electricity is the energy used that makes the bulb's light shine. Its ability to light up your surrounding is similar to the light within you. Through meditation, you expand your light, which gives expansion to your awareness. As you do, you feel God's universal loving healing energy flow through you in abundance. It activates your godly qualities, balancing and aligning you with its power. This loving energy is the electricity and the nervous system being the element. The grace and flow of this loving energy through you will depend on how bright your inner light shines. When there is a good connection, the light shines brightly. However, if there is an interruption in the connection, this will cause a blockage in the flow and the inner light becomes dim. For some people it may appear to be completely out.

Refer to *Sura 24 Verses 35-36; Sura 6 Verse 1; Sura 57 Verses 12-13;* and *Sura 66 Verse 8.*

If you look up the word 'niche' in the Oxford Encyclopaedic English Dictionary, you will find the following explanations.

A shallow recess in a wall to contain a statue.
A comfortable or suitable position in life or employment.
An appropriate combination of conditions for a species to thrive.

The former verses are parables about the light. Our world is a small recess, a heart in our solar system. As you begin to expand your awareness, you will realise that the conscious self is a niche within the subconscious self; which is within the unconscious; within the super conscious. You can keep applying this understanding and expression all the way back to God, as you travel through the varying degrees of light, as you raise your state of consciousness.

To create a niche for our world there was a shift in time and space. This created a bubble effect. It is within this space we exist. An example in this physical reality is similar to the animals that live in water. For some animals, water is their only home whereas others have adapted to living on land as well. Some evolve and take to the air, spending the final stage of their life in flight. For example, a dragonfly spends the first part of its life living underwater. Then, it emerges, and goes through a transformation as it breaks out of its skin and takes to the air for the final stage of its physical journey. You are like a dragonfly but you do not know it yet. Meditation gives you an opportunity to live and enjoy life in a variety of worlds but you have to learn to adapt.

The light of the Earth is not only talking about the physical sun in the sky. Your mind is the Earth and when you close your eyes, the light you see within is the face of God. Our Earthly sun, its heat and light help to sustain life on Earth. The light you see within gives life and sustenance to your body, mind and spirit self. The glass of the lantern is symbolic of the bubble effect that separates spirit and matter. It is the veil between the two worlds. It is there, yet it is not there. Some people can hear and see through the veil, other people cannot. Our light is like a brilliant star but our enclosure into limited time and space causes our perception of the light to be lesser than it is. There is a divine light residing within each one of us. Through our godly qualities, we can build the light we see into a full flame. When the love expands, it lights the flame within. As you build up your light, it shines on the parables of *The Holy Quran*. As you build your light, *The Quran* will reveal to you the secrets it holds.

Living life in loving surrender is the magical way that opens the door to Heaven. A part of the teaching of the prophets was to explain to us that a miracle is no more than the interplay of forces using energy, sound and light. People who are able to do what you call miracles are aware of the inner light that flows around and through them. Some people have the ability to materialise, construct, dematerialise or alter the form of matter. Be aware of the thought processes that are taking place within you. You have to learn to make your thoughts work for you; you should not work for your thoughts.

Energy

Energy follows thought, sound is its vibration and light is the expression of energy and sound. As we travel, we create energy and willpower, sound and thinking, light and form to give us our reality. We know that the kinds of thought we entertain are partly because of our leaning in the mind.

Each of us connects to God through a loving life force. We reflect back to God all that is within ourselves. As we reflect within and send energy out, we began to see within ourselves the developmental growth of our own inner light. Through our life and during our meditations, the energy we call inspiration is impressed on us. It suggests to us in a loving way the truths we need to hear. Through inspiration, we receive information and mystical knowledge about matters we previously did not know. We become aware of our own ability to manifest. The fact that you have choice and can independently create thoughts will make you aware of this.

As we enter the light, we become aware of a presence within it. We look at God knowing we were a part of this magnificent being. When we look at each other, we are aware of God's divine light existing within all things and sustaining and giving life to all. As we express the essence of ourselves, through the recognition of our godly qualities, we became aware of our own innate divine spiritual qualities. We became aware that we live within God, as we experience His universal life force sustaining, flowing through us and ever around us.

'Go forth and multiply' and this is exactly what we have done. Trillions and trillions of spirit particles scattered themselves throughout God's creation.

All shapes and forms created are made of varying densities of energy, sound and light. Surrounding all creation, there is a loving energy. It is for us to express this loving fragrance. As we do, we become aware of the greater part of ourselves.

As you expand your light, you will realise, as a reality, that there are other worlds besides the one you see with the physical eyes. As we go out exploring the vastness of what God created, we inhabit many of the different planets in and beyond this universe. Each planet's inhabitants are cloth in a form and density consistent with its planet's vibrational structure and atmosphere, which is not always visible to our physical eyes.

Sound

The love between God and His creation produces a vibration, a frequency, a sound, a note. From each spirit being there is also emitted a vibration according to its inner manifestations. As the notes come together, a melody manifests within the heart of God. Within each of us there is created a melody by which we communicate. Allow yourself to stand within your inner centre of light and communicate with love. Realise how bright and shining a star you are, how beautiful the melody is that comes to you from the heart centre of your inner sanctuary.

It is during our explorations that distortions appear within us. We began to go out of alignment with the absolute. Those whose note and energy has remained aware and attuned to God in surrender send forth loving thoughts that are followed by a gentle wind. Their energy vibration has not fallen out of alignment with the truth. Their prayers, filled with love ascend up to the heavens. They are answered with the greatest consideration. The loving energy sent back as a reply activates their light force. They receive that which is sent from the heavens and work to fulfil their duty.

As the lost became knowledgeable of those in the greater states of awareness, each will learn from the other. The person in the physical will learn something about life in the hereafter and those in the hereafter will gain an understanding about the human condition. For more clarification read *Sura 2 Verses 31-33*. Remember the story when God taught Adam things that the angels had no knowledge of. We do indeed learn from each other. Through inspiration, the person in the physical world is able to find a balance. They are then able to raise their consciousness above the ideas that caused them mischief. It is important to remember that each child born, is an explorer of the universe and has arrived in the land to experience what it has to offer, in order that it might grow in awareness. Your children do not belong to you like property. They have come into this world as a part of their own spiritual journey and development.

As the explorers awakened to the melody of their greater self, they learnt wisdom during their inner visitation to the sacred mosque. They clothe what they find in words to help balance and heal other explorers they met in the lands they visited.

It is through your inner communication that the door to the hereafter remains open. This allows a steady stream of inspiration to flow directly from the spiritual and became a foundation within you. Through you, God's truth establishes itself in the land. Those who pay attention to their inner wisdom are able to use it to elevate themselves. God's streams of information are open to everyone and not only a selected few.

Through the communication and establishment of knowledge between the two worlds, many people who became lost will re-kindle their inner light. They will recognise and know how inspiration imprints itself on them. They begin to follow the divine path of wisdom as they start to awaken to their true inner self. They will meet up with people who retained knowledge of the spiritual truths to re-learn and realign themselves. They then become the cherisher of this divine knowledge and flow with a favourable wind. They raise their consciousness beyond the vehicle that they inhabit. They become explorers of both the physical and the spiritual realms.

Because of the diverse communities that sprang up, as the explorers of the universes scattered themselves, many teachers are sent to each community to establish teachings and give guidance. They come with a single message of love that has never changed.

Light

Our expression of energies and sounds of love come together within us to create a light. As the light radiates out, it will heal and soothe you.

The knowledge that you hold and its vocal expression alone, will not ensure you a grand position in the hereafter. Even the darkness can present to you a flowery discourse. Knowledge comes and goes but love is a life force that will always exist. In the world, you have to work to maintain love's expression. Love overrides all knowledge. Look at what people will endure for love. They will give freely of themselves, for love is not fleeting but is a constant loving energy you can manifest. Love creates a light. In love and light, you ascend to Heaven.

One of the reasons why we crave love so much is because love is a divine expression of our inner self. God's love adds to our love, giving us an experience of completeness. Love is the energy produced but not the fuel. Love is the expression of the feeling of your spirit. Yet, you are not the love. It is another godly quality you are able to manifest in the same way there are other parts to your personality, yet unlike these parts of yourself, love has the greatest depth, breadth and width. God created love so that we, using our own intelligence, might prefer to choose love, working with the Spiritual Laws, to find our way home to the heavens.

You will know yourself that before you can feel love within yourself you have to create the intention to manifest love. Outer things may excite you into manifesting some expressions of love within yourself. However, you are the one who opens the door to the manifestation of love. The outer is but a trigger for what exists within you already.

What we call darkness is not a negative force but a force created to balance creation. At first, it was a very subtle energy but as more beings entered new creations to gain experiences through physical matter structures, they generated irregular manifestations as they turned from God. With the creation of irregularity there came into existence limitation. We enter physical bodies and we will have to keep on entering new creations until we have transformed all that we have created in error.

Each time you express an idea, you know yourself where it came from. Between our polarity, we experience duality as we each move around our own house according to our choice. Based on your decision, the Spiritual Laws impress on you a balance according to your manifest expression. All things manifest because you bring them forth. You allow them to expand and grow to become a force within yourself. When it is but a thought in your mind, it is at a distance from the physical world. When it becomes a spoken word or an act, you are the one who brings forth what you create and you let it enter the world as an expression.

Raise your consciousness and see all life through the eyes of love. Let yourself attune to the loving energies that are all around you. Allow them to shape your perception of the world. When you arrive at the door of the place you leaned towards, it will open and let you in. Familiarise yourself with yourself. You are energy, you are sound and you are light. The more love you create and allow to flow through you, when you take your leave and go back home, greater will be the love where you will dwell.

Look to that special part of God within you, that place of inner love and solitude. This is the place where you will find God's face. It is always present and smiling at you. On your inner foundation of loving energy, sound and light, stands your inner mosque. Repeat this affirmation to help you see God's face.

Energy, sound and light
Within my heart unite.
Create a sacred space
That I may see God's face.

Chapter 19: All Things Are Recorded

The Christians and Hindus mystics call the record of deeds, The Akashic Records. In *The Quran*, the same hall of records is as follows.

Sura 83 Verses 7 and 18
7. Nay! Surely the record of the wicked is (preserved) in Sijjin.
18. Nay, verily the record of the righteous is (preserved) in 'Illiyin.

Other related verses are as follows, giving you an understanding that a record is kept about all that takes place in this world. It is from your record that you are apportioned an amount.

Read *Sura 6 Verse 59*. This verse goes on to say, *(inscribed) in a record clear (to those who can read)*.

In this context, also read, *Sura 17 Verse 13.*

Sura 17 Verse 36
36. For every act of hearing or of seeing, or of (feeling in) the heart will be enquired into.

This library of records is accessible. This place is one of the many places along the path of love. God grants you visitation rights in order that a matter may be resolved or revealed. Some of the things that you see prepare you for future tasks along the pathway of your life.

It is surrounding this area of understanding that many people are reaping what they have sown. It is in their forgetfulness of their past deeds that they thrust on other people, with great determination, condemnation and blame, the negative emotional content of their inner self.

Study *The Quran*, do not rely on hearsay. For people who deliberately transgress beyond the bounds and rightful laws, greater harm they do to themselves. It is not for you to mix yourself up in their affairs. In time, they will return and they must learn to heal their own self through love, trust and truth. You will find that life is a school and there is always a need for you to look at the way you are acting during your lessons. Are you improving yourself or are you swept along by a harsh wind? Do you read the book of enlightenment for yourself, or instead do you follow conjecture and the will and desires of others?

Sura 57 Verse 22
22. No misfortune can happen on Earth or in your souls but is recorded in a decree before we bring it into existence.

Refer to *Sura 2 Verse 26*. Everyone is capable of separating error from truth. However, there are people who choose to ignore the inner message. Doing so, they miss the opportunity to rekindle their flame of light. Each morning and evening of each day, go into your inner world glorifying the name of God. Stand firmly in the light. A part of this light will remain with you after you have done your work. Each time you enter your house, you know you have the opportunity to reach the station of Abraham where you will find security. What separates Heaven from Hell is a state of consciousness neither here nor there. Let your inner vision detect the place you must cross over into the light.

The prayers of the doubtful people amount to nothing more than the whistling and the clapping of hands. Their belief system of partial truths gives them but a partial view. They are on the receiving end of their own thoughts and actions, as the Law of Cause and Effect plays itself out in their life? Reach beyond the glamour of the world of form. Work to change yourself and those around you will change. It is in your small changes that the truth has an opportunity to flourish.

When you learn something new, let it replace what you do not need. What you do not know, or cannot do, does not mean it cannot exist or is impossible. It is a matter of expanding your awareness until you know. When you do not know the answer to something, in the light above waits the answer. Let yourself surrender to the truth and trust and you will gain access to the answers you seek.

Read *Sura 83 Verses 6-9* and *Sura 83 Verses 18-20*. Why, you may ask yourself, does *The Quran* keep referring to, those who can read? There is a library in the hereafter that contains all knowledge. As you express love, you open your awareness. Love transforms you and God grants you access to places previously inaccessible to you. Knowledge from the eternal library becomes accessible to you. You realise this because it imprints images, signs and symbols, seen by you through your mind's eye. You will come to know that the laws perfect their order for the Earth two days before the manifest event. You are indeed among those who are learning how to see clearly. This same library, also known as The Akashic Records contains information about this world and everything that has ever happened. Everything you have ever thought, every feeling within your heart is contained therein. See *Sura 17 Verse 36*. In the physical world, it is easy to manipulate history. The eternal record holds true every moment. Refer to *Sura 5 Verse 51*.

What is here is not new. It is a confirmation of what has gone before it. You will find in all the other religions, there are books about meditation. Each religion brings forth beautiful words of wisdom, each sharing a common thread. The truth has always been here but the irregularities have covered your vision of it. You will see them fighting, squabbling and bickering among themselves. Speaking from your inner wisdom encourages those around you to try a little harder. Your brain is for you to use, not so other people can use it for you. You can compare the mind faculty to a mirror that reflects images. There are many images imprinted on the screen of the mind. People who are observant follow what they feel to be true. Pay attention to what you see within, more than what you hear from other people. God wants you to follow the truth and trust that comes to you. All that is here is but to inspire you to seek your own inner understanding. Do not rely too much on other people but listen and pay attention to what inspires you. That which comes to you in love, comes from God. In the end, your return is to the hereafter and the foundation on which you built yourself.

In giving your mind over to somebody else, you dis-empower yourself. By handing the control of your life over to someone else, you are taking that responsibility for your own inner self's development away from yourself. All that other people experience is for them. All that you experience is for you. It is not for you to live your life according to the experiences, desires and will of someone else. It is for each of us to strive for our own freedom. You will find that as you reside within, you must choose between those who will elevate you and those who will drag you down. Irregularities say; 'This is from God' but God does not have such intentions or motives behind the construction of such thoughts as they produce.

The Spiritual Laws surround all things that exist in the Heavens and the Earth. How you understand and work with the laws in your life depends on you. The laws men make in the physical world serve a purpose. Greater are the laws that guide and govern us spiritually. Abide by the laws of the material world. Live by the laws of the spiritual. Doing this you will get the best of both worlds. Do not look at other people and think; 'If they can, I can'. Each of us receives what we need. This shows how unique we each are and how precisely the laws work. If anyone refuses to follow the inspiration and expand the love within, it is to their own loss. Refer to *Sura 5 Verse 48.*

Many people associate their life's situations with the way they feel other people treat them, without looking at how they are processing events in their lives. We hardly ever check to see if our knowledge about a matter is correct. God is not responsible for what you go through, neither is Iblis, the Devil, Satan. You always have a choice. You have lived before and the memories of your passed actions are stored in the eternal record. From these records you are apportioned an amount. Do you transform your portion into light? Alternatively, do you remain surrounded by your irregularities? Because reaping through physical action and reaction must run its course, the information in the record of deeds is not readily available to everyone.

Sura 20 Verse 124
124. But whosoever turns away from my message verily for him is a life narrowed down.

Be open to change. Refusing to give up old ideas will not slowdown the process of change. You will be left in the past, repeatedly living history instead of being a history maker. Through the expression of love, you will become a history maker as you step into a new flow of energy. You can raise yourself out of the past and into the future. Eventually, God plucks you from the world to be re-educated and relocated. When called to account, your falsehoods will leave you as the truth makes itself known.

Sura 17 Verse 14
14. (It will be said to him): Read thy (own) record: Sufficient is thy soul this day to make out an account against thee.

If you do not strive to expand, there will always be a lacking in your understanding. The former verse tells us something remarkable about ourselves. God does not judge you in the way you believe. You make an account against yourself. In the hereafter, when you see the record of your deeds, you will judge yourself. Your comparison will be against the divine plan that you agreed to follow before you came to this physical world.

As you lean in the mind one way or another, you will feel a presence and influence. As you express love, you enter the flow and guidance from the Heavens. Sit in meditation and enter the flow of this loving influence. Once connected to the flow, you will begin to feel and hear more, extracting a greater amount of wisdom contained therein.

What you now pass over was at one time necessary in your life. You have indeed raised your station since the last time you were here. Think about what we said about remote viewing. If we must learn to command a sight of all things, surely God commands a greater sight. Repeat this affirmation to be with God.

I am in God and God's light is in me.
In the light of my soul, God's light rise up in me.
You are in God and God's light is in you.
In the light of your soul, God's light rise up in you.
All are in God and God's light is in all.
In the light of all souls, God's light rise up in all.

Sura 18 Verse 49
49. They will say, 'Ah! Woe to us! a book is this! It leaves out nothing small or great, but takes account thereof!'

Read, *Sura 30 Verses 43-44.* The spreading of your *'couch of repose'* is through the expansion of your loving awareness as it spreads out. *Sura 20 Verses 25-26*, was expressed by Moses, when he asked God to; *'expand his breast'.* The couch on which you rest is your loving surrender, trust and truth. It does not matter which of the religions you follow or do not follow. The most important thing to remember, is to act out of love. Put all the love you can into what you do. The degrees of how much you trust God, shows the strength of your true belief.

Sura 50 Verse 17
17. Behold two (Guardian angels) appointed to learn (his doings) learn (and note them) one sitting on the right and one on the left.

Climb away from the collection of falsehoods that have built up around you. Your material circumstances are not going to change drastically by remembering to pray, remembering to meditate. You may not pay much attention to your thoughts in this life but in the next world, you will not be able to hide your content and its expression. By raising yourself beyond the reach of the irregular thoughts in your mind, you will move closer to your inner sacred mosque.

You have to overcome your negative emotions and fears. Recognise that we are all one big spiritual family. You cannot live as 'them' and 'us'. In a situation of them and us, each side is like the waves in an ocean as it swells up and pushes out its chest in pride. The words of truth that enter the tribal self of each side become twisted and distorted, then swallowed up and devoured and spat back in a rage of hatred. Be aware of those whose speech comes from the tribal self. They are indeed mischief-makers in the land. It does not have to be like this. Visualise yourself connecting and flowing along a beautiful expression of love. Use your ability to reason and act on the best thoughts that enter your mind. No other except God, can supply you with the love you seek.

Read *Sura 10 Verse 45,* which is about how we will recognise each other in the hereafter. Why only have a belief when real knowledge and experiences are available to you? For those who expand their feelings and listen to their inner voice of love and wisdom, they will come to know, this voice is true guidance. That they receive inspired thoughts from their Guardian angels. The lost people are those who do not accept the wisdom of the small voice of truth that is advising them. Instead, they allow the tribal bully to take control of their life. Behind their laughter, there is but doubt and sorrow at what they have said and done. They changed the words that came in truth, creating and following something other than what comes to aid them on their journey. Their self-doubts soon grow to establish themselves as irregularities. Strive to become what is pleasing and god like. Scale the heights of spiritual development, live and share your life. By sharing with other people, you will raise your consciousness. In the next world, you will carry on living and sharing your life with the people you love and care for. Remember, life in the next world is all about love, service, harmony and balance. Learn to harmonise your life with all people. Realise they too are on their pathway and they may not be much different from you. Some of the best advice you can give is to encourage someone to do it with love.

To help you get an idea about where you stand in the great scheme of things, let us take three different viewpoints. Thoughts from the evolved self, memory related thoughts that show up in the conscious self and thoughts from the tribal self. Let us say they came in the form of; 'if this, that or the other'. The difference in your nearness to God depends on which thought process you decided to follow, as each direction opens a different door. Use what arises within to clarify to yourself your station and nearness to God. Ask yourself; 'Are you in a state of loving surrender?' You should not find any matter too difficult to make a decision about. The harder it is for you to make a decision, the further you could be from your goal. If you surrender and put other people before yourself, it takes but moments to settle the matter. If you put yourself first, you may find yourself playing with the ideas or scenarios, tossing and turning them like pancakes, seeking the best advantage. Follow the best of your thoughts and be aware of which direction you surrender.

You can reside in the dwellings on high, while still in the physical body. As you travel; 'them' and 'us' becomes; 'we', 'we' belonging to all and all belongs to God. Ask yourself now and again; 'Which side of the dividing line do I reside in?' Look for the light through the eyes of love and you will find the face of God. Be a good student of life, a student of unconditional love and exceptional learning. The verses of *The Quran* are like an ocean where many swimmers play. Take to the ocean and learn to become a stronger swimmer.

Meditation allows you to swim beyond the waves that wash other people back to the old land.

Become an active participant in the spreading of light. Seek the love within yourself and see yourself for the person you really are. You are energy, sound and light. You are an explorer. You are beautiful and have the potential to become greater than you could ever imagine. Seek the face of God. As you do, you will come to know God. He shows Himself to you as a light. You can feel His loving energy around you. When you enter the light, you are indeed standing in the presence of God. Leave the land where you dwell and climb to the higher ground.

Sura 39 Verse 21
21. Seest thou not that God sends down rain from the sky, and leads it through springs in the Earth?

Much of the spiritual energy that flows into our world reaches us through energy vortexes. The Islamic name is *latifs*. Christians and Hindus know them as chakras. There are different energy vortexes at certain points in different locations around the Earth. The key words in the former verse are; *'springs in the Earth'*. Within our human and spiritual bodies, there is an alignment of spiritual energy centres. For the human being, there are seven major centres of energy, which transcend into a white light. You could think of them as the rainbow of the spirit. These colours and their physical or mental attributes from the bottom up, as listed below.

The Rainbow of the Spirit

- Red – physical.
- Orange – the nervous system.
- Yellow – emotional.
- Pink or green – feeling.
- Blue – mental.
- Indigo - higher mental.

- Violet – the soul.
- White – the higher soul.

These seven chakras in the physical body run in a straight line down the centre of the body. They start above the crown of your head, running down the centre to the genital area. Many books written about the chakras also include information about the minor chakras as well. It is for you to go out into the world and seek out more knowledge about them. They are introduced here to bring them to your awareness.

Sura 21 Verse 80
80. It was we who taught him the making of coats of mail for your benefit, to guard you from each other's violence: Will ye then be grateful?

Also read, *Sura 34 Verse 11.* The first of these two verses come from a story about Solomon. The second verse is from a story about David. Both verses explain that there is a need to make a 'coat of mail' to protect yourself. In the olden days, soldiers wore coats of mail during battle. These coats were made of rings of metal linked together. Here you can see how a spiritual matter of great importance can relate to a material dress sense. *The Quran* is making you aware that you need to create something that will protect you and as you do, balance well the rings of chained armour.

Your coat or aura radiates with different colours, like the coat of many colours told in the Biblical story of Joseph. We each have an aura. An aura is a field of energy that extends itself around each of us. Each person's aura changes colour, according to their inner expression and will. During your daily interactions, you deplete yourself of energy. To help keep you energised, you are able to retract your auric field back into yourself.

Read *Sura 74 Verse 4.* Meditation allows you to cleanse your aura using visualisation. You can work with your aura, setting it up as a force-field of protection that automatically repels irregularities and unwanted energies. Your spirit body and its aura is the garment of your inner self in the afterlife. When you visualise yourself filling with light, you are indeed cleaning your spiritual garments.

Read *Sura 16 Verse 48.* It is from this verse that you will realise all things have an energy field, an aura. Loving feelings expand your aura and different thoughts change its colour. You see it arcing and swirling around you in prostration. Do not let your aura fill with dark spots. By detecting someone's energy field, you can know in what manner, they prostrate themselves before God. You can recognise this by the way you feel when you are around certain people. Some people give you an unpleasant feeling, whereas other people make you happy. You notice their energy as your energy goes out before you.

The expression of good thoughts takes away the control that self-sabotaging thoughts try to exert over you. When your vision of perfection swerves and you lose focus, you believe what God sends to you in life is not perfect. It is for you to bring your vision into line with God's vision for your life. Only when you believe all is perfect will you start to align yourself with perfection.

Your vision of perfection comes from your own version of perfection. How will you ever see perfection if you are always complaining about its ordered sequence? It is your task to align yourself with the loving streams of energy from the Heavens. They will bring your vision back into focus with the inner truth.

If you do not emotionally express yourself in certain ways when surrounded by certain circumstances, do not feel your heart is cold. Are your inner core beliefs transcending that of the emotional self? Love and understanding sustain you. Your internal reference to life depends on what you accept as truth. As you hold yourself steady in the light, having built your life on love, trust and truth, the favourable winds along which you flow will carry you to a place where you will have peace of mind, safety and security. This means that the emotional outbursts others create around you will not drive you into despair. Hold on to your faith, hold on to your belief. On your inner journey, you remain steadfast without swaying. You hold yourself steady as you swim beyond the ocean of emotion from the moon.

When you accept the truth, the understanding you gain about matters sustains you during what would have otherwise been a difficult situation. Remember, there is your truth according to material matters and there is the spiritual truth. Each can give you a different view of life. Feelings are in degrees closer to the truth. Learn to put your feelings before your emotions. By transforming your negative emotions, you will become more than you were. As you transform yourself, your fears and insecurities born out of your emotions will transform into light. This will lighten, brighten and strengthen you. Let your feelings be your guide. Challenge and change the thoughts that show up in your mind and work to remain in the light.

In the name of God, most Gracious, most Merciful.
Wa alaikum as-salam, my brothers and sisters.

Made in the USA
Monee, IL
21 March 2023